Diet recommendations for fatty liver

Please check these recommendations always with a nutrition consultant, therapist, doctor or dietician. The recipes and the list of ingredients are supporting the conventional medical therapy.
The calorie disclosures of fresh ingredients (fruit and vegetables) vary according to quality and time of harvest. The contents were checked by a dietician and a nutrition consultant for the Traditional Chinese Medicine (TCM).

Author:
©2019 Josef Miligui
www.ebns.at

Source:
The lists are created from the EBNS database for nutritional counseling. The database is used by dietitians, therapists and doctors for advising the patient / client.

Literature:
The specialist literature and the training documents of the German and Austrian dietary and traditional Chinese medicine serve as a knowledge base. We have used the documents as a basis of knowledge, adapted it to our experience and completed them.
http://di-book.com

Production and publishing:
BoD – Books on Demand, Norderstedt
ISBN: 9783746043104

Diet recommendations for DIETETICS - Gastrointestinal tract - Liver, gallbladder, bile ducts - Fatty liver

1   Treatment strategy

High-quality protein, light normal diet.
Drink at least 2 liters daily.
Avoid alcohol, trans fat. Avoid large portions and fat meals. Avoid foods

rich in fructose and starch.
Observe normal blood glucose levels.

2   Avoid

Alcohol, fat food.

3   Breakfast

kkal. per serving

Apple - banana cream 110
Banana Soymilk 125
Barley and vegetable soup 281
Barley mash with plums 106
Barley soup 265
Breakfast - Rice with fruits 230
Breakfast with cheese 593
Carrot and potato rucola sandwich 94
Carrot and rice gruel soup 101
Cereal fruit pulp 175
Compote from rhubarb 48
Corn coffee with cardamom 3
Cottage cheese with steamed fruit 214
Couscous Salad 338
Cranberry juice 43
Cranberry yogurt mix 57
Cucumber soup 95
Curry rice with raisins and nuts 275
Delicately spiced zucchini with tomatoes 203
Fish soup with rosemary 271
Frozen pineapple juice 29
Fruit juice 175
Grated apple 120
Grated carrots with apple 74
Hungarian rice salad 421
Kohlrabi in chervil sauce with potatoes 187
Lettuce with vinegar dressing 67
Oat flakes with aromatic spices 280
Potato cream with herbs and fresh cheese 217
Potato-basil soup 95
Pumpkin-yoghurt soup 68
Rhubarb and apple jelly 180
Rice congee with honey pear and black sesame 158
Ricepudding 316

4 Snack

5 Lunch

8   Any time

9   Recipes

(rec.) = You can use more.
(little) = You should use less than specified
(no) omit.

9.1   Andalusian fish pot

Strengthens immune system, prevents cancer, dissolves stagnation, promotes weight loss. Good to fight immunodeficiency, loss of appetite, flatulence, high blood pressure, depressions, diabetes, diarrhea, stimulates appetite.
Cooking time approx. 30 min
Allergens: ADLO
4 portions to 355g. / 348kcal. - (carb:71% / prot:29%)
100g.=97,96kcal. / protein 20,03g. fat:6,51g.
µg. - Ph:3,89 Na:5,05 Ka:8,67 Mg:3,36 Ca:10,73 Fe:0,03 Zn:0,02 Col.:0,79 Hsr.:2,47

Quantity of ingredients:
Basic recipe for a vegetable soup (nutritious) 2 cups / 500g. (yes)
Onion (spring onion) 2 pieces / 40g. (yes)
Olive oil 1 table spoon / 20g. (yes)
Lemon peel 1/2 piece / 3g. (yes)
Bay leaf 1 piece / 1g. (yes)
Potato 5/8 oz / 200g. (yes)
Cod 3/4 lbs / 300g. (yes)
White wine 4 table spoons / 80g. (little)
Lemon juice 1/2 teaspoon / 10g. (yes)
Salt 1 pinch / 1g. (little)
Pepper (ground) 1 pinch / 0,2g. ()
Parsley 1 table spoon / 15g. (yes)
White bread (wheat bread) 8 slices / 250g. (little)

Cooking instructions:
Boil the vegetable broth with small spring onion, olive oil, grated lemon peel and bay leaf. Boil covered for 10 minutes. Add the peeled, diced potatoes and boil in about 8 minutes. Add fish pieces and white wine and switch to small heat. In the slightly boiling broth put the fish and boil it a few minutes. Season with lemon juice, salt and pepper. Serve with parsley sprinkled.
White bread as a side dish.

9.2   Antipasti

Improves blood circulation, anti-inflammatory, relieves pain. Diuretic, promotes digestion, reduces blood pressure. antioxidative, antibacterial, affects anorexia, improves digestion, flatulence, stomach weakness, stimulating.
Cooking time approx. 40 min
3 portions to 246,67g. / 100kcal. - (carb:54% / prot:46%)
100g.=40,54kcal. / protein 2,74g. fat:5,6g.
µg. - Ph:7,93 Na:1,08 Ka:67,54 Mg:5,14 Ca:7,21 Fe:0,24 Zn:0,03 Col.:0 Hsr.:5,8

Quantity of ingredients:
Pepperoni 1 piece / 5g. (yes)
Lemon juice 1 table spoon / 10g. (yes)
Aubergine 1 piece / 300g. (yes)
Tomato 4 pieces / 200g. (yes)
Zucchini 5/8 oz / 200g. (yes)
Lemon peel 1/2 piece / 3g. (yes)
Olive oil 1 table spoon / 15g. (yes)
Basil (fresh) 8 leaves / 5g. (yes)
Salt 1 pinch / 0,5g. (little)
Coriander 1/2 teaspoon / 2g. (yes)

Cooking instructions:
Preheat the oven to 250 degrees Celsius and bake the hot peppers until the bowl becomes dark (about 20 minutes). Cover the hot peppers with a clear film and allow to cool. Peel the skin and cut into strips about 2 cm wide. Cut tomatoes in half and spread with oil in slices of aubergine and bake in the oven at 200 degrees golden brown (about 10 minutes) Fry the zucchini slices in the grill pan (without fat).
Mix everything together, mix the marinade of olive oil, salt and lemon peel and pour over the vegetables, sprinkle with coriander. Leave for 1 hour.

9.3   Apple - banana cream

Regulates gastrointestinal function, provides vitamin C, cholesterol lowering, reduces inflammation, diuretic, improves blood circulation.
Cooking time approx. 15 min
4 portions to 206,25g. / 110kcal. - (carb:94% / prot:6%)
100g.=53,45kcal. / protein 0,84g. fat:0,51g.
µg. - Ph:0,75 Na:0,12 Ka:9,5 Mg:0,68 Ca:0,56 Fe:0,03 Zn:0,01 Col.:0 Hsr.:0,8

Quantity of ingredients:
Apple (sour) 7/8 lbs / 400g. (yes)
Water 3/4 cup - 6 oz / 200g. (yes)
Lemon peel 1/2 piece / 2g. (yes)
Sugar brown 2 teaspoons / 6g. (little)
Cinnamon sticks 1 piece / 0g. (yes)
Banana 1 piece / 150g. (yes)
Acerola fruit nectar or powder 1 teaspoon / 2g. (little)
Orange juice 1/2 piece / 50g. (little)
Lemon juice 1 table spoon / 10g. (yes)

Cooking instructions:
Cut the apple into fine slices, bring water to boil and add the apple slices, orange- and lemon peel, sugar and cinnamon and simmer about 7 minutes. The apples should be almost soft. Remove acerola and the cinnamon stick. Mix the apple, the banana, the orange juice and the lemon juice.

9.4   Artichoke soup

Detoxifying, supports urination, regulates digestion, stimulates appetite, gentle laxative, forcing spleen, promotes weight loss. Strengthens gastrointestinal function, expands blood vessels, prevents cancer.
Cooking time approx. 40 min
Allergens: GLN
3 portions to 243,67g. / 142kcal. - (carb:60% / prot:40%)
100g.=58,41kcal. / protein 3,3g. fat:10,01g.
µg. - Ph:18,58 Na:43,88 Ka:39,61 Mg:18,21 Ca:61,23 Fe:0,28 Zn:0,03 Col.:0,73
Hsr.:11,24

Quantity of ingredients:
Artichoke 4 pieces / 400g. (yes)
Butter organic 1 table spoon / 20g. (little)
Onion (shallot) 1 piece / 20g. (yes)
Corn flour 1 table spoon / 10g. (yes)
Nutmeg 1 pinch / 0,5g. (yes)
Basic recipe for a vegetable soup (nutritious) 1 cup / 250g. (yes)
Salt 1 pinch / 0,5g. (little)
Lemon 1/4 piece / 8g. (yes)
Lemon peel 1/4 piece / 1g. (yes)
Turmeric (yellow root) 1 pinch / 1g. (rec.)
Sesame, white 1 teaspoon / 10g. (yes)

Cooking instructions:
Boil the artichokes in 2 liters of water with salt until the outer leaves are light removable. Remove leaves and flower center (fibrous) so that only the soil remains.
Melt the butter, cut the onion into small pieces and steam gently; add some cornmeal, nutmeg; brew with vegetable soup; add salt, a little lemon peel and juice, turmeric and artichoke bottoms, cook gently and puree; Season with Tahin and sprinkle with sesame before serving.

9.5 Asparagus and herb ragout

Diuretic, improves blood circulation, prevents cancer, dissolves stagnation, promotes weight loss. Good to fight immunodeficiency, loss of appetite, flatulence, high blood pressure, depressions, diabetes, diarrhea, stimulates liver function.
Cooking time approx. 30 min
Allergens: GL
4 portions to 465,5g. / 168kcal. - (carb:78% / prot:22%)
100g.=36,14kcal. / protein 7,54g. fat:4,09g.
µg. - Ph:2,55 Na:0,54 Ka:11,94 Mg:2,69 Ca:9,45 Fe:0,06 Zn:0,02 Col.:0 Hsr.:1,09

Quantity of ingredients:
Basic recipe for a vegetable soup (nutritious) 2 cups / 500g. (yes)
Lemon peel 1/2 piece / 3g. (yes)
Coriander 1/4 teaspoon / 1g. (yes)
Nutmeg 1 pinch / 0,3g. (yes)
Asparagus (green or white) 1,8 lbs / 800g. (yes)
Parsley 1 Bunch / 125g. (yes)
Crème fraiche cheese 2 table spoons / 30g. (little)
Lemon juice 1 teaspoon / 3g. (yes)
Potato 7/8 lbs / 400g. (yes)

Cooking instructions:
Cook potatoes with plenty of salted water about 20 min. until soft.
Heat the vegetable stock with lemon zest, coriander and nutmeg till it boil. Cook the peeled and sliced asparagus in it.
Drain asparagus in a sieve. Collect the cooking liquid.
In the blender mix 200 g of cooked asparagus (the lower ends), cooking liquid and parsley to a smooth sauce. Beat the sauce with crème fraîche until smooth. Add asparagus and heat again and season with lemon juice, salt and pepper. Serve with the potatoes.

9.6   Banana Soymilk

Good to fight loss of appetite, oral mucosa inflammation. Strengthens body energy, promotes stomach-spleen harmony, promotes digestion, regulates gastrointestinal function. Relieves pain, detoxifying, bactericide.
Cooking time approx. 5 min
Allergens: E
2 portions to 263g. / 126kcal. - (carb:60% / prot:40%)
100g.=47,72kcal. / protein 7,49g. fat:4,13g.
µg. - Ph:10,97 Na:125,56 Ka:55,04 Mg:6,65 Ca:4,89 Fe:0,2 Zn:0,11 Col.:0 Hsr.:16,84

Quantity of ingredients:
Banana 1 piece / 120g. (yes)
Soybean milk 1 1/2 cups / 400g. (yes)
Honey 1 teaspoon / 3g. (little)
Cinnamon ground 1 pinch / 1g. (yes)
Acerola fruit nectar or powder 1 teaspoon / 2g. (little)

Cooking instructions:
Cut the banana into pieces, puree them with soy milk, acerola, honey and cinnamon with the mixing stick.

9.7   Barley and vegetable soup

Supports urination, detoxifying, promotes spleen and liver, reduces blood pressure, strengthens immune system, prevents cancer, reduces radiation damage, promotes digestion, helps to digest fat, harmonizes metabolism.
Cooking time approx. 2 hours
Allergens: AGL
3 portions to 304g. / 281kcal. - (carb:73% / prot:27%)
100g.=92,54kcal. / protein 11,93g. fat:5,74g.
µg. - Ph:9,75 Na:1,36 Ka:21,85 Mg:3,27 Ca:3,09 Fe:0,14 Zn:0,08 Col.:0,09 Hsr.:9,52

Quantity of ingredients:
Barley 1 cup / 120g. (yes)
Shiitake, dried 1/8 oz / 4g. (yes)
Onion (shallot) 1 piece / 20g. (yes)
Cumin (Caraway seed) 1 knife tip / 0,5g. (yes)
Sunflower oil 1 table spoon / 10g. (yes)
Water 1 cup / 250g. (yes)
Celery sticks 2 branches / 20g. (yes)
Peas, green 5/8 lbs - 8oz / 250g. (yes)
Tomato 1 piece / 50g. (yes)

Carrot 2 pieces / 150g. (yes)
French beans Handful / 30g. (yes)
Salt 1 pinch / 1g. (little)
Pepper (ground) 1 pinch / 0,5g. ()
Parsley 1 teaspoon / 3g. (yes)
Butter organic 1 teaspoon / 3g. (little)

Cooking instructions:
Soak the barley in the evening for the next day. Soak the mushrooms separately at the next day. Brown onion and cumin in oil, then boil with water. Add the chopped vegetables, some salt, the barley and the shiitake mushrooms and cook everything to a thick soup. At the end, season with pepper, parsley and a little butter.

9.8 Barley mash with plums

Promotes spleen, diuretic, forcing spleen, supports urination, relaxes, reduces internal heat.
Cooking time approx. 25 min
Allergens: AG
5 portions to 289,6g. / 107kcal. - (carb:81% / prot:19%)
100g.=36,88kcal. / protein 3,15g. fat:1,57g.
µg. - Ph:1,2 Na:0,1 Ka:2,2 Mg:0,44 Ca:0,34 Fe:0,01 Zn:0,01 Col.:0,04 Hsr.:0,42

Quantity of ingredients:
Water 10 cups / 1200g. (yes)
Barley 1 cup / 120g. (yes)
Plum 1 cup / 120g. (yes)
Butter organic 2 teaspoons / 6g. (little)
Sugar cane sugar 1/2 teaspoon / 2g. (little)

Cooking instructions:
Grind coarse the barley and roast it dry. Add hot water, add ginger and cardamom and let it swell to a pulp in low heat. Core the plums and boil for 10 minutes with a little water. At the end, add the stewed plums, a little butter and sweetener.

Variant: If you want to go fast, you can use barley flakes instead of shot.

9.9 Barley soup

Diuretic, forcing spleen, supports urination, stimulates liver function, antioxidative, promotes digestion, detoxifying, reduces blood lipids, stimulates, dissolves stagnation.
Cooking time approx. 25 min
Allergens: A
2 portions to 201g. / 265kcal. - (carb:76% / prot:24%)
100g.=131,84kcal. / protein 8,16g. fat:6,42g.
µg. - Ph:28,03 Na:2,36 Ka:51,88 Mg:9,52 Ca:8,33 Fe:0,31 Zn:0,22 Col.:0 Hsr.:8,81

Quantity of ingredients:
Barley 1 cup / 120g. (yes)
Salt 1 pinch / 1g. (little)
Ginger fresh 1/2 teaspoon / 1g. (yes)
Olive oil 1 table spoon / 10g. (yes)
Parsley 3 table spoons / 30g. (yes)
Water 1 1/2 cups / 240g. (yes)

Cooking instructions:
Roast the barley in the pan, then grind it to the ground, and boil with water, some salt and ginger to a mash. Before
serving add oil and parsley.

Variant: You can add a better taste to the dish if you cook it with prepared vegetable or meat broth.

9.10 Basic recipe for a beef broth (clear)

Strengthens muscles, tendons and bones, reduces blood pressure, strengthens immune system, prevents cancer, reduces radiation damage, stimulates digestion, reduces pain, promotes digestion, diuretic. Rosemary stimulates digestion.
Cooking time approx. 4-8 hours
Allergens: O
10 portions to 276g. / 114kcal. - (carb:22% / prot:78%)
100g.=41,41kcal. / protein 12,22g. fat:4,09g.
µg. - Ph:0,51 Na:0,31 Ka:1,34 Mg:0,11 Ca:0,25 Fe:0,01 Zn:0,01 Col.:0,14 Hsr.:0,36

Quantity of ingredients:
Beef soup meat 1,1 lbs / 500g. (yes)
Beef meatbones 5/8 oz / 200g. (yes)
Vinegar (Red wine vinegar) 1 dash / 3g. (yes)
Juniper berry 8 pieces / 6g. (yes)

Rosemary 1 pinch / 1g. (yes)
Carrot 3 pieces / 210g. (yes)
Parsnip 2 pieces / 300g. (yes)
Leek 1 piece / 200g. (yes)
Ginger fresh 1/2 teaspoon / 5g. (yes)
Lovage 1 stem / 15g. (yes)
Clove 2 pieces / 2g. (yes)
Pimento 6 pieces / 12g. (yes)
Anise (Common Fennel) 2 pieces / 1g. (yes)
Salt 1 teaspoon / 5g. (little)
Water 3,3 lbs / 1300g. (yes)

Cooking instructions:
Heat water, a dash of red wine vinegar, some juniper berries, a little rosemary, bones and meat till it boils; add carrot, parsnip, leek, ginger, lovage, clove, allspice, star anise and a little salt; simmer for 4-8 hours then strain.
Refrigerate for later use.

9.11 Basic recipe for a chicken broth worming

Strengthens blood, strengthens bone marrow, reduces blood pressure, strengthens immune system, prevents cancer, reduces radiation damage, promotes sweating, dissolves stagnation, good to fight loss of appetite, flatulence.
Cooking time approx. 2-3 hours
Allergens: L
9 portions to 244,89g. / 90kcal. - (carb:10% / prot:90%)
100g.=36,66kcal. / protein 15,68g. fat:11,56g.
µg. - Ph:0,86 Na:0,59 Ka:1,87 Mg:0,13 Ca:0,38 Fe:0,01 Zn:0 Col.:0,25 Hsr.:0,92

Quantity of ingredients:
Chicken meat 1/2 piece / 600g. (yes)
Carrot 2 pieces / 150g. (yes)
Leek 1 stick / 45g. (yes)
Celery root 1 piece / 500g. (yes)
Ginger fresh 2 slices / 2g. (yes)
Juniper berry 1 teaspoon / 3g. (yes)
Bay leaf 3 pieces / 2g. (yes)
Water 4 cup / 900g. (yes)

Cooking instructions:
Remove chicken parts from fat. Place chicken pieces in a saucepan with hot water and heat till it boils briefly, skimming any resulting foam. Add coarsely chopped vegetables and all spices and cook over medium heat for 2 to 3 hours. Strain the finished soup. Throw away vegetables and bones.
Tip: If you want to use the meat as a soup insert, take out after 45 minutes and return only the bones in the soup.
Refrigerate for later use.

9.12 Basic recipe for a duck broth

Forcing spleen, strengthens blood, supports urination, reduces blood pressure, strengthens immune system, prevents cancer, reduces radiation damage.
Cooking time approx. 2-3 hours
Allergens: L
6 portions to 241,67g. / 61kcal. - (carb:22% / prot:78%)
100g.=25,38kcal. / protein 10,16g. fat:4,86g.
µg. - Ph:1,63 Na:1,95 Ka:5,7 Mg:0,3 Ca:1,1 Fe:0,03 Zn:0,01 Col.:0,77 Hsr.:2,29

Quantity of ingredients:
Duck (heart) 5/8 oz / 200g. (yes)
Water 2 cup / 450g. (yes)
Duck (slaughtered) 1/4 lbs - 4oz / 100g. (yes)
Carrot 2 pieces / 100g. (yes)
Celery root 1/2 piece / 600g. (yes)

Cooking instructions:
Cook duck pieces with vegetables for 2-3 hours. Sift broth through a fine sieve and refrigerate for later use.

The innards can be reused: You cut them finely and leaves them for a few minutes with fresh vegetables in the broth draw. Sprinkle with parsley before serving.

9.13 Basic recipe for a fish broth

Strengthens the kidneys, promotes watering, reduces blood pressure, strengthens immune system, prevents cancer, reduces radiation damage. Low in cholesterol and protein rich. Improves blood circulation, stimulates appetite.
Cooking time approx. 40 min
Allergens: DLO
5 portions to 243,8g. / 128kcal. - (carb:34% / prot:66%)
100g.=52,34kcal. / protein 9,81g. fat:5,2g.
µg. - Ph:14,91 Na:7,09 Ka:31,5 Mg:2,39 Ca:4,63 Fe:0,11 Zn:0,02 Col.:0,01 Hsr.:11,94

Quantity of ingredients:
Fish pieces mixed (fresh water) 3/4 lbs / 300g. (yes)
Celery root 1/4 lbs - 4oz / 120g. (yes)
Leek 2 inches / 10g. (yes)
Carrot 2 pieces / 150g. (yes)
White wine 1/2 cup / 125g. (little)
Lemon 1/2 piece / 50g. (yes)
Bay leaf 2 leaves / 2g. (yes)
Peppercorns 3 pieces / 2g. (yes)
Olive oil 1 table spoon / 10g. (yes)
Water 2 cup / 450g. (yes)

Cooking instructions:
Fry celery, chopped carrots and leeks in olive oil, add bay leaf and peppercorns, add pieces of fish and sauté briefly. Add water, add little white wine or lemon. Simmer gently for 30 minutes. Skim off the resulting foam several times. In the end, sift the ingredients through a cloth.
Refrigerate for later use

9.14 Basic recipe for a reissue soup (Congee)

Low fat content, for the drainage of the body overweight and high blood pressure.
Cooking time approx. 2-4 hours
3 portions to 273,33g. / 140kcal. - (carb:90% / prot:10%)
100g.=51,34kcal. / protein 2,96g. fat:0,48g.
µg. - Ph:1,95 Na:0,19 Ka:1,67 Mg:1,14 Ca:0,57 Fe:0,01 Zn:0,02 Col.:0 Hsr.:2,11

Quantity of ingredients:
Rice variety any 1 cup / 120g. (yes)
Water 6 cups / 700g. (yes)

Cooking instructions:
Cook rice and water in a ratio of about 1: 6. The amount of water determines the thickness of the mash (matter of taste).
Put the rice in a saucepan with a heavy lid. It is important to simmer the rice after a short boil on the slightest flame, otherwise it burns.
Boil the rice for 2-4 hours. The longer he cooks, the more he strengthens.
If you want to eat the dish for breakfast, you can put the rice on just before bedtime.
To be on the safe side, you should first check the behavior of your pot and cooker under observation for a similar amount of time, so that nothing burns.
Refrigerate for later use.

9.15 Basic recipe for a vegetable soup, nutritious

Reduces blood pressure, strengthens immune system, prevents cancer, forcing spleen, dissolves stagnation, promotes weight loss. Good to fight immunodeficiency, high blood pressure, depressions, diabetes, diarrhea, reduces blood lipids.
Cooking time approx. 2-3 hours
Allergens: L
5 portions to 240,6g. / 48kcal. - (carb:71% / prot:29%)
100g.=19,87kcal. / protein 1,56g. fat:1,31g.
µg. - Ph:0,97 Na:0,73 Ka:5,14 Mg:0,36 Ca:1,26 Fe:0,02 Zn:0,01 Col.:0 Hsr.:0,56

Quantity of ingredients:
Olive oil 1 table spoon / 4g. (yes)
Onion white 1 piece / 60g. (yes)
Carrot 3 pieces / 200g. (yes)
Parsnip 3/8 lbs - 6oz / 150g. (yes)
Celery root 1 cup / 100g. (yes)
Ginger fresh 1/2 teaspoon / 2g. (yes)
Lemon 1/2 piece / 25g. (yes)
Juniper berry 6 pieces / 6g. (yes)
Thyme dried 1 pinch / 1g. (yes)
Lovage 1 table spoon / 3g. (yes)
Bay leaf 2 leaves / 1g. (yes)
Salt 1 pinch / 1g. (little)
Water 3 cups / 650g. (yes)

Cooking instructions:
Cut the vegetables into cubes.
Heat oil in hot pot, fry shortly onions and vegetables.
Add cold water, then add ginger, bay leaf and lemon juice.
Season with juniper, thyme and lovage. Cover for 2 - 3 hours on a low heat and simmer.
The used vegetables should be thrown away.
The basic recipe serves as a soup base and to refine vegetables, legumes or cereals.
If you want to eat vegetable soup immediately, add the desired vegetables half an hour before.
Refrigerate for later use.

9.16 Basmati rice + Zucchini tofu dish

Diuretic, supports urination, harmonizes spleen and stomach, reduces flatulence, good to fight body overweight and high blood pressure.
Antioxidative, promotes digestion, perspiration, reduces blood lipids, forcing spleen.
Cooking time approx. 20 min
Allergens: E
4 portions to 306,75g. / 146kcal. - (carb:57% / prot:43%)
100g.=47,51kcal. / protein 7,95g. fat:4,89g.
µg. - Ph:13,21 Na:0,7 Ka:33,77 Mg:10,99 Ca:11,98 Fe:0,34 Zn:0,02 Col.:0 Hsr.:7,75

Quantity of ingredients:
Soy Tofu 5/8 lbs - 8oz / 250g. (yes)
Olive oil 2 table spoons / 6g. (yes)
Coriander 1/2 teaspoon / 4g. (yes)
Ginger fresh 1/2 teaspoon / 4g. (yes)
Rice Basmati 1/2 cup / 60g. (yes)
Water 3 cups / 200g. (yes)
Zucchini 1 piece / 700g. (yes)

Cooking instructions:
Cut tofu cubes and marinate with olive oil, tamari, crushed coriander and ginger. Leave at least 1 hour.
Cook Basmati rice with the water. You can season with onion and cardamom.
Roast zucchini and tofu in pan in the hot oil for approx. 5-7 min.
Serve rice and tofu on a plate.
Add the parsley.
Can also be used as a salad for the home and on the go.

9.17 Beef pumpkin and vegetable stew

Reduces inflammation, improves digestion, strengthens the muscles, tendons and bones, promotes digestion, helps to digest fat.
Cooking time approx. 1 hour
Allergens: AL
4 portions to 403,75g. / 369kcal. - (carb:48% / prot:52%)
100g.=91,46kcal. / protein 30,38g. fat:11,37g.
µg. - Ph:4,56 Na:3,23 Ka:16,05 Mg:1,7 Ca:3,71 Fe:0,08 Zn:0,08 Col.:1 Hsr.:2,83

Quantity of ingredients:
Beef meat 3/4 lbs / 350g. (yes)
Pumpkin 3/4 lbs / 350g. (yes)
Leek 3/8 lbs - 6oz / 150g. (yes)
Potato 3/4 lbs / 350g. (yes)
Tomato 3/8 lbs - 6oz / 150g. (yes)
Olive oil 2 table spoons / 25g. (yes)
Basic recipe for a vegetable soup (nutritious) 1/4 lbs - 4oz / 125g. (yes)
Salt 1 pinch / 1g. (little)
Pepper (ground) 1 pinch / 0,5g. ()
Sugar cane sugar 1 pinch / 1g. (little)
Parsley 1/2 bunch / 30g. (yes)
White bread (wheat bread) 4 slices / 80g. (little)

Cooking instructions:
Dice beef. Peel pumpkin and dice. Cut the leek into rings and dice the peeled potatoes.
Brew the tomatoes with boiling water, peel off the skin and dice.
Steam the meat in olive oil and fill with vegetable stock. Add the cleaned vegetables. Season with salt, pepper, paprika, cumin and fructose.
Stew for 30 minutes over low heat.
Season again and sprinkle with parsley and serve with white bread.

9.18 Black root with yogurt

Stimulates kidney, bladder and forces the cleaning of the body. In the physiological sense, they generally stimulate the glands in the organism. Good to fight acute or chronic constipation of the intestine.
Rich in Vitamins and trace elements.
Cooking time approx. 20 min
Allergens: AG
2 portions to 304,5g. / 319kcal. - (carb:77% / prot:23%)
100g.=104,76kcal. / protein 7,98g. fat:2,08g.
µg. - Ph:22,7 Na:23,23 Ka:67,95 Mg:6,53 Ca:15,06 Fe:0,64 Zn:0,11 Col.:0,16 Hsr.:14,42

Quantity of ingredients:
Salsify 1 lbs / 400g. (yes)
Yogurt (natural, 1.5% fat) 4 table spoons / 80g. (yes)
Salt 1 pinch / 1g. (little)
Multi-grain bread (gray bread) 6 slices / 120g. (yes)

Cooking instructions:
Peel the salsify and simmer in salted water until tender. Pour away the water, cool the salsify and cut it to size. Cover with yoghurt and sprinkle with fresh herbs. Serve with the bread.
You can also use the salsify from the conserve.

9.19 Breakfast - Rice with fruits

Good to fight blood circulation disorders, thrombose, risk of embolism, high blood pressure, a headache, heart attack and stroke. Encourages blood build-up, promotes digestion, reduces Inflammation.
Cooking time approx. 10 min - 3 hours
Allergens: GHO
3 portions to 282g. / 231kcal. - (carb:90% / prot:10%)
100g.=81,8kcal. / protein 3,59g. fat:7,61g.
µg. - Ph:3,19 Na:0,7 Ka:8,57 Mg:20,72 Ca:21,22 Fe:0,05 Zn:0,02 Col.:0,54 Hsr.:0,92

Quantity of ingredients:
Basic recipe for a rice soup (Congee) 6 cups / 500g. (yes)
Cow's milk (whole milk 3.5% fat) 1/2 to 1 cup / 80g. (yes)
Honey 1 table spoon / 10g. (little)
Butter organic 1 table spoon / 15g. (little)
Dates dried 1 table spoon / 15g. (little)
Fig 1 table spoon / 15g. (yes)
Apple (sour) 1 piece / 200g. (yes)
Hazelnuts 1/2 teaspoon / 5g. (yes)
Almond 1/2 teaspoon / 5g. (yes)
Cinnamon ground 1 pinch / 1g. (yes)

Cooking instructions:
Cook rice congee according to basic recipe or use pre-cooked.
Make it with the milk more fluid and sweeter with honey.
Fry the fruits and nuts in butter and mix with the finished rice soup, add chopped dates, figs and the apple.

9.20 Breakfast with cheese

Good to fight weakness, stomach pressure, belching, diabetes, acute or chronic obstruction of the bowel, skin problems. Coffee supports urinating, stimulates appetite, detoxifying, increases blood glucose levels, harmonizes heart rhythm.
Cooking time approx. 10 min
Allergens: AGO
1 portion to 364g. / 593kcal. - (carb:46% / prot:54%)
100g.=162,91kcal. / protein 22,49g. fat:34,96g.
µg. - Ph:139,8 Na:214,1 Ka:121 Mg:21,93 Ca:99,75 Fe:0,82 Zn:1,12 Col.:10,93 Hsr.:18,97

Quantity of ingredients:
Water 1 cup / 120g. (yes)
Coffee 2 teaspoons / 4g. (yes)
Margarine 1/2 oz / 10g. (little)
Edam cheese 1 oz / 30g. (yes)
Strawberry jam 1/2 oz / 20g. (little)
Curd cheese 20% 1/8 lbs - 2oz / 40g. (yes)

Cooking instructions:
Prepare coffee as usual. Avoid sugar or use sweetener. Cover the bread slices with margarine and put the cheese and marmalade on the breakfast table. Decorating decoratively increases your appetite.

9.21 Broccoli cream soup

Strengthen your immune system, build and maintain healthy bones, teeth, hair and nails. Reduces blood pressure, strengthens immune system, prevents cancer, reduces radiation damage.
Cooking time approx. 30 min
Allergens: LO
6 portions to 251,17g. / 98kcal. - (carb:79% / prot:21%)
100g.=39,02kcal. / protein 4,17g. fat:1,91g.
µg. - Ph:1,14 Na:0,45 Ka:4,37 Mg:1,39 Ca:5,42 Fe:0,03 Zn:0,01 Col.:0 Hsr.:0,45

Quantity of ingredients:
Olive oil 2 table spoons / 7g. (yes)
Broccoli 1,1 lbs / 500g. (yes)
Carrot 2 pieces / 150g. (yes)
Potato 2 pieces / 120g. (yes)
Onion white 1 piece / 50g. (yes)
Water 1 cup / 50g. (yes)
Basic recipe for a vegetable soup (nutritious) 2 cup / 500g. (yes)

White wine 1/2 cup / 125g. (little)
Sage 1 teaspoon / 2g. (yes)
Rosemary 1 teaspoon / 2g. (yes)
Pepper (ground) 1 pinch / 0,5g. ()
Salt 1 pinch / 1g. (little)

Cooking instructions:
Add the olive oil to the pan, add the washed and cut broccoli, diced carrots and potatoes, sauté for a short time, add the chopped onion, fill with water, enough water to cover the vegetables at least 3 finger breadths. Add bouillon, salt, add a little bit of white wine, add the seasoned sage and rosemary.
Heat till it boils and then simmer on a small fire for about 25 minutes.
Season with pepper, if necessary season with sea salt. Purée the soup.

9.22 Carrot and millet bake with apple compote

Promotes spleen and liver, reduces blood pressure, strengthens immune system, prevents cancer, reduces radiation damage, calms nerves and stomach, diuretic, good to fight chronic constipation of the intestine.
Cooking time approx. 1 hour
Allergens: CGH
7 portions to 347,86g. / 350kcal. - (carb:64% / prot:36%)
100g.=100,53kcal. / protein 12,54g. fat:12,54g.
µg. - Ph:1,79 Na:0,66 Ka:2,7 Mg:0,54 Ca:1,07 Fe:0,03 Zn:0,01 Col.:0,83 Hsr.:0,28

Quantity of ingredients:
Millet 5/8 oz / 200g. (yes)
Cow's milk (whole milk 3.5% fat) 2 cups / 450g. (yes)
Lemon peel 1/2 piece / 2g. (yes)
Sugar brown 2 table spoons / 20g. (little)
Carrot 7/8 lbs / 400g. (yes)
Ginger fresh 2 teaspoons / 6g. (yes)
Acerola fruit nectar or powder 1 teaspoon / 2g. (little)
Almond puree 1/8 lbs - 2oz / 50g. (yes)
Chicken egg 4 pieces / 240g. (yes)
Yogurt (natural, 1.5% fat) 3/8 lbs - 6oz / 150g. (yes)
Butter organic 1 teaspoon / 4g. (little)
Apple (sour) 4 pieces / 600g. (yes)
Water 1 cup / 300g. (yes)
Clove 2 pieces / 1g. (yes)
Sugar brown 1 table spoon / 10g. (little)

Cooking instructions:
Preheat the oven to 100°C/212°F (with circulating air 8o°C/176°F, gas level 2).
Heat the milk with the millet till it boils, add lemon zest and sugar. Cover and simmer for 5 minutes, then simmer in a preheated oven for 20 minutes. Switch oven to medium heat.
Peel apples and cut into small pieces, boil with water, cloves and sugar for about 5 minutes.
Mix the millet in a bowl with the grated carrots, finely chopped ginger and acerola.
Mix the almond paste (or butter) with the hand mixer. Add egg yolk and stir everything to a smooth cream. Mix in sour cream. Add millet and carrots.
Beat the egg whites very stiff and lift them under the millet pulp. Brush out a baking dish with butter. Add the millet and bake in a preheated oven for 45 minutes on a low heat.
Serve with the apple compote.

9.23 Carrot and potato rucola sandwich

Reduces inflammation, improves digestion, supports urination, lowers cholesterol, strengthens immune system, prevents cancer, good to fight constipation (Fibre-rich), dissolves stagnation.
Cooking time approx. 20 min
Allergens: AG
4 portions to 116,25g. / 94kcal. - (carb:55% / prot:45%)
100g.=80,86kcal. / protein 2,68g. fat:2,83g.
µg. - Ph:4,15 Na:4,56 Ka:16,7 Mg:1,23 Ca:1,78 Fe:0,06 Zn:0,03 Col.:0,25 Hsr.:1,27

Quantity of ingredients:
Potato (mealy) 5/8 oz / 200g. (yes)
Carrot 1 piece / 50g. (yes)
Sour cream 15% fat 3 table spoons / 45g. (little)
Onion (spring onion) 1 piece / 20g. (yes)
Rucola 1/2 bunch / 100g. ()
Lemon peel 1/4 teaspoon / 1g. (yes)
Salt 1 pinch / 1g. (little)
Pepper (ground) 1 pinch / 0,2g. ()

Cooking instructions:
Cook the potatoes gently, peel and squeeze through the potato press.
Cook vegetable broth according to the basic recipe and remove a carrot after a short cooking time and finely crush with a fork.
Stir the potatoes, carrots, grated lemon zest and sour cream into a

smooth cream. Mix carrot and potato cream with finely chopped rocket salad. Season the spread with salt and pepper and spread the bread. Sprinkle with the finely chopped young onions.

9.24 Carrot and rice gruel soup

Stops diarrhea, good to fight fever, strengthens immune system, reduces blood pressure.
Cooking time approx. 10 min
1 portion to 224g. / 101kcal. - (carb:96% / prot:4%)
100g.=45,09kcal. / protein 2,37g. fat:0,4g.
µg. - Ph:27,48 Na:20,34 Ka:65,63 Mg:170,89 Ca:178,57 Fe:1,03 Zn:0,34 Col.:0 Hsr.:12,3

Quantity of ingredients:
Basic recipe for a rice soup (Congee) 1 cup / 120g. (yes)
Carrot 2 pieces / 100g. (yes)
Salt 1 teaspoon / 4g. (little)

Cooking instructions:
Peel and grate carrots. Heat the rice soup (according to the basic recipe) till it boils and add the grated carrots and salt. Cook for 10 minutes.

9.25 Celery and potato cream soup

Reduces blood pressure, strengthens immune system, promotes weight loss. Good to fight immunodeficiency, loss of appetite, flatulence, depressions, diabetes, diarrhea, improves digestion.
Cooking time approx. 45 min
Allergens: GL
4 portions to 241,5g. / 113kcal. - (carb:83% / prot:17%)
100g.=46,69kcal. / protein 2,15g. fat:5,52g.
µg. - Ph:5,96 Na:3,46 Ka:23,98 Mg:22,27 Ca:83,51 Fe:0,18 Zn:0,01 Col.:0 Hsr.:1,49

Quantity of ingredients:
Olive oil 1 table spoon / 10g. (yes)
Onion white 1/2 piece / 25g. (yes)
Basic recipe for a vegetable soup (nutritious) 3 cups / 700g. (yes)
Potato 5/8 oz / 200g. (yes)
Nutmeg 1 pinch / 0,5g. (yes)
Ground 1 pinch / 0,5g. (yes)
Lemon peel 1/4 piece / 1g. (yes)
Crème fraiche cheese 2 table spoons / 20g. (little)
Salt 1 pinch / 1g. (little)
Parsley 1 table spoon / 8g. (yes)

Cooking instructions:

Heat the olive oil in a saucepan lightly. Fry the onions very gently in a mild heat. Pour with vegetable stock according to the basic recipe. Cover and cook for 15 minutes.

Add curd-cut potato, celery, nutmeg, cumin and lemon zest. Spice with salt and cook for 12 minutes. Potatoes and celery should be soft. Remove the lemon peel.

Puree the soup with crème fraiche using a blender. Season the soup with salt.

Arrange the soup in portions with the chopped parsley.

9.26 Cereal fruit pulp

Lots of vitamin C, strengthens immune system, antiparasitic.
Cooking time approx. 10 min
Allergens: A
1 portion to 215g. / 175kcal. - (carb:71% / prot:29%)
100g.=81,4kcal. / protein 2,7g. fat:6,92g.
µg. - Ph:41,51 Na:2,49 Ka:91 Mg:16,16 Ca:10,4 Fe:0,66 Zn:0,47 Col.:0 Hsr.:21,3

Quantity of ingredients:

Oat flakes (whole grain) 1/2 oz / 20g. (yes)
Water 3,5 oz / 90g. (yes)
Apple juice (natural cloudy) 1/4 lbs - 4oz / 100g. (little)
Rapeseed oil 1/8 oz / 5g. (yes)

Cooking instructions:

Heat the water till it boils the add the cereals. Instant flakes you only need to mix with hot water. Stir fruit juice or puree and grease. The fresh fruit (for example, apples, pears, peaches) can be raw or kneaded. Frozen fruit or industrially produced fruit jars without added sugar are also suitable. Bananas should be mixed with less sweet fruit.

9.27 Chicken soup with egg yolk and parsley

Strengthens blood, strengthens bone marrow, reduces blood pressure, strengthens immune system. Parsley stimulates liver function, harmonizes liver and spleen, strengthens eyesight, detoxifying.
Cooking time approx. 10 min
Allergens: CL
2 portions to 260g. / 118kcal. - (carb:82% / prot:18%)
100g.=45,19kcal. / protein 16,35g. fat:2,49g.
µg. - Ph:6,98 Na:8,83 Ka:9 Mg:24,79 Ca:69,4 Fe:0,28 Zn:0,05 Col.:6,52 Hsr.:2,22

Quantity of ingredients:
Basic recipe for a chicken soup (warming) 2 cup / 500g. (yes)
Chicken yolk 1 piece / 10g. (yes)
Parsley 1 table spoon / 10g. (yes)

Cooking instructions:
Cook the chicken broth according to the basic recipe.
Heat broth and bubble the egg yolk. Sprinkle the chopped parsley over it and let it rest for about 2 minutes. Drink in small sips.

9.28 Compote from rhubarb

Antipyretic, analgesic, detoxifying, bactericide.
Cooking time approx. 15 min
1 portion to 230g. / 48kcal. - (carb:92% / prot:8%)
100g.=20,87kcal. / protein 0,64g. fat:0,1g.
µg. - Ph:11,22 Na:1,7 Ka:119,43 Mg:6,43 Ca:25,43 Fe:0,28 Zn:0,15 Col.:0 Hsr.:2,61

Quantity of ingredients:
Rhubarb 1/4 lbs - 4oz / 100g. (yes)
Water 1 cup / 120g. (yes)
Honey 1 table spoon / 10g. (little)

Cooking instructions:
Wash rhubarb and cut small. Boil in the water. Allow to cool a little and add the honey.

9.29 Corn coffee with cardamom

Diuretic, forcing spleen, supports urination, relaxes, reduces fat.
Cooking time approx. 5 min
1 portion to 136g. / 3kcal. - (carb:99% / prot:1%)
100g.=2,21kcal. / protein 0,11g. fat:0,08g.
µg. - Ph:1,29 Na:1,02 Ka:7,9 Mg:2,49 Ca:5,37 Fe:0,08 Zn:0,09 Col.:0 Hsr.:0

Quantity of ingredients:
Cereal coffee 1 table spoon / 15g. (yes)
Cardamom 2 cores / 1g. (yes)
Water 1 cup / 120g. (yes)

Cooking instructions:
Boil water, coffee, sugar and cardamom. Let it set for one min before drinking.

9.30 Cottage cheese with steamed fruit

Good to fight loss of appetite, promotes digestion, supports urination.
Cooking time approx. 20 min
Allergens: G
2 portions to 250g. / 214kcal. - (carb:40% / prot:60%)
100g.=85,8kcal. / protein 18,45g. fat:6,4g.
µg. - Ph:22,3 Na:57,25 Ka:25,45 Mg:1,85 Ca:12,8 Fe:0,05 Zn:0,09 Col.:0,64 Hsr.:1,5

Quantity of ingredients:
Cottage cheese 3/4 lbs / 300g. (yes)
Apple (sour) 1 piece / 100g. (yes)
Pear 1 piece / 100g. (yes)

Cooking instructions:
Wash apples and pears well, do not peel, and chop small. In a pot with
steam filter, boil them al dente, remove and allow to cool down.
Serve the cheese, spread the fruit on it.

9.31 Couscous Salad

Prevents cancer, forcing spleen, promotes digestion, stimulates liver
function, reduces blood pressure, strengthens immune system, reduces
radiation damage, diuretic.
Cooking time approx. 25 min
Allergens: A
3 portions to 285,67g. / 338kcal. - (carb:75% / prot:25%)
100g.=118,32kcal. / protein 12,21g. fat:7,11g.
µg. - Ph:5,1 Na:5,76 Ka:27,89 Mg:2,17 Ca:7,1 Fe:0,15 Zn:0,07 Col.:0 Hsr.:4,56

Quantity of ingredients:
Water 1 cup / 100g. (yes)
Olive oil 1 table spoon / 15g. (yes)
Couscous 5/8 oz / 200g. (yes)
Lemon juice 3 table spoons / 30g. (yes)
Lemon peel 1 teaspoon / 2g. (yes)
Tomato 2 pieces / 80g. (yes)
Cucumber 1/4 lbs - 4oz / 100g. (yes)
Carrot 1/4 lbs - 4oz / 100g. (yes)
Parsley 1 Bunch / 100g. (yes)
Chives 1 Bunch / 100g. (yes)
Peppermint 3 twigs / 30g. (yes)

Cooking instructions:
Boil in a small saucepan 250 ml. water with salt and 1 tablespoon olive oil. Add the couscous, take the stove in the front and let it swell covered for 5 minutes. Put the couscous back on the stove and let it simmer for about 2 minutes with gentle stirring. If necessary, add 1 - 3 tbsp of hot water.
Mix the couscous with lemon juice, chopped lemon peel and 1 tbsp oil, season with salt and pepper and leave to set.
Add couscous with tomatoes, cucumber, parsley (all diced), carrots (grated), chives and mint (finely chopped). Season the couscous salad with lemon juice, salt and pepper.

9.32 Cranberry juice

Antibacterial, good to fight loss of appetite, arteriosclerosis, bladder infections, diarrhea, colds. Antipyretic, against free radicals, gout, diuretic, stomach ulcers, oral mucosa inflammation, rheumatism.
Cooking time approx. 5 min
1 portion to 160g. / 43kcal. - (carb:98% / prot:2%)
100g.=26,88kcal. / protein 0,14g. fat:0,02g.
µg. - Ph:2,06 Na:1,53 Ka:11,69 Mg:1,16 Ca:4,22 Fe:0,09 Zn:0,09 Col.:0 Hsr.:3,12

Quantity of ingredients:
Cranberries 2 table spoons / 25g. (yes)
Water 1 cup / 125g. (yes)
Honey 1 table spoon / 10g. (little)

Cooking instructions:
Mix the cranberries with a little water with the blender to a pulp. Add the remaining water and sweeten with the honey.

9.33 Cranberry yogurt mix

Good to fight acute or chronic constipation of the intestine, oral mucosal inflammation, diarrhea, flatulence, throat irritation.
Cooking time approx. 5 min
Allergens: GO
2 portions to 197,5g. / 57kcal. - (carb:75% / prot:25%)
100g.=28,86kcal. / protein 2,13g. fat:1,02g.
µg. - Ph:7,17 Na:5,87 Ka:13,16 Mg:2,71 Ca:16,61 Fe:0,01 Zn:0,03 Col.:0,39 Hsr.:0,2

Quantity of ingredients:
Yogurt (natural, 1.5% fat) 1/4 lbs - 4oz / 125g. (yes)

Cooking instructions:
Mix yoghurt, cranberry jam and mineral water until frothy.

9.34 Cucumber soup

Diuretic, detoxifying, suppresses conversion of sugar into fat, lowers cholesterol, prevents cancer, promotes digestion, diaphoretic, dries out, good to fight yeast infections.
Cooking time approx. 20 min
Allergens: M
4 portions to 235,25g. / 96kcal. - (carb:22% / prot:78%)
100g.=40,6kcal. / protein 0,91g. fat:9,03g.
µg. - Ph:2,67 Na:1,28 Ka:15,6 Mg:1,17 Ca:2,57 Fe:0,06 Zn:0,01 Col.:0 Hsr.:0,85

Quantity of ingredients:
Olive oil 2 table spoons / 35g. (yes)
Cucumber 2 pieces / 400g. (yes)
Water 2 cup / 500g. (yes)
Sage 3 leaves / 3g. (yes)
Coriander 1 pinch / 1g. (yes)
Cardamom 1 pinch / 1g. (yes)
Salt 1 pinch / 1g. (little)

Cooking instructions:
Heat oil and roast short the small cucumbers. Add Mustard seeds, coriander, cardamom and salt. Add water. Simmer for 10-15 min. Puree and decorate with fresh chopped sage.

9.35 Curry rice with raisins and nuts

Stops diarrhea, promotes digestion, appetizing, harmonizes the stomach, improves blood circulation, improves medication effect, stimulates appetite, detoxifies the skin, stimulates nerves, frees breathing, increases body temperature, promotes perspiration.
Cooking time approx. 30 min
Allergens: HO
4 portions to 291g. / 275kcal. - (carb:76% / prot:24%)
100g.=94,59kcal. / protein 3,78g. fat:8,87g.
µg - Ph:12,77 Na:2,26 Ka:25,36 Mg:5,82 Ca:3,11 Fe:0,14 Zn:0,02 Col.:0 Hsr.:4,85

Quantity of ingredients:
Sunflower oil 1 table spoon / 15g. (yes)
Onion white 1 piece / 50g. (yes)
Curry 1/2 teaspoon / 2g. (yes)
Rice wild (nature rice) 1 cup / 120g. (yes)

Salt 1 pinch / 1g. (little)
White wine 1/2 cup / 125g. (little)
Lemon Alternatively for white wine / g. (yes)
Apple (sweet) 2 pieces / 300g. (yes)
Raisins 2 table spoons / 25g. (little)
Walnuts 2 table spoons / 25g. (yes)
Water 6 cups / 500g. (yes)

Cooking instructions:
Heat oil in a pot; fry chopped onions until glassy; add the curry and let it
foam for a short time; then fry the raw rice for a few minutes over a
gentle heat, stirring constantly; Salt, a dash of white wine or lemon
juice, rose paprika, sweet apples chopped, raisins, chopped, roasted
nuts added; pour hot water on it until well covered; simmer until the rice
is cooked.

Goes well with: carrot and fennel vegetables, legumes with boiled
vegetables, sliced poultry with ginger and mushrooms.

9.36 Delicately spiced zucchini with tomatoes

Diuretic, promotes digestion, helps to digest fat, reduces blood
pressure, dissolves stagnation, antioxidative, supports urination,
diuretic, warming the body from the inside, expands blood vessels.
Cooking time approx. 10 min
4 portions to 396,5g. / 203kcal. - (carb:72% / prot:28%)
100g.=51,2kcal. / protein 5,38g. fat:6,62g.
µg. - Ph:10,4 Na:0,79 Ka:35,33 Mg:6,3 Ca:5,58 Fe:0,26 Zn:0,02 Col.:0 Hsr.:5,53

Quantity of ingredients:
Olive oil 1 table spoon / 20g. (yes)
Onion white 2 pieces / 120g. (yes)
Zucchini 4 pieces / 800g. (yes)
Oregano dried 1 pinch / 1g. (yes)
Basil (fresh) 6-8 leaves / 3g. (yes)
Salt 1 pinch / 1g. (little)
Tomato 2 pieces / 120g. (yes)
Rice (whole grain) 1 cup / 120g. (yes)
Water 6 cups / 400g. (yes)
Salt 1 pinch / 1g. (little)

Cooking instructions:
In a hot pan, fry olive oil, finely chopped onions and finely chopped zucchini until half cooked. Add plenty of dried oregano. Salt and chop the tomatoes for a few minutes until the zucchini are tender but crisp. Add fresh basil as desired.

Variation: Put some sheep's cheese over the tomatoes and finish cooking with the lid closed.

Place the rice in salted water, heat till it boils and let it simmer over low heat for about 15 minutes.

9.37 Exotic lenses

Strengthens heart and kidney, diuretic, calms the stomach, promotes digestion, dissolves stagnation, helps to digest fat, supports urination, reduces blood pressure, stimulating the immune system.
Cooking time approx. 45 min
Allergens: NO
4 portions to 273,25g. / 144kcal. - (carb:71% / prot:29%)
100g.=52,61kcal. / protein 5,82g. fat:3,45g.
µg. - Ph:13,57 Na:11,6 Ka:48,37 Mg:8,53 Ca:8,91 Fe:0,27 Zn:0,02 Col.:0 Hsr.:13,4

Quantity of ingredients:
Sesame oil 1 table spoon / 10g. (yes)
Onion white 2 pieces / 120g. (yes)
Ginger fresh 1/2 teaspoon / 2g. (yes)
Thyme dried 1/2 teaspoon / 1g. (yes)
Cumin (Caraway seed) 1/2 teaspoon / 2g. (yes)
Lentils red 1 cup / 120g. (yes)
Wakame 1 inch / 1g. (yes)
Lemon 1/2 piece / 20g. (yes)
Bocksdorn fruits (Fructus Lycii, goji berry dried 2 pinches / 2g. (yes)
Sugar cane sugar 1 pinch / 1g. (little)
Chili (pod or ground) 1 pinch / 0,5g. (yes)
Salt 1 pinch / 1g. (little)
Vinegar (Apple vinegar) 1/2 teaspoon / 1g. (yes)
Tomato 1 piece / 50g. (yes)
Chard 5/8 oz / 200g. (yes)
Cauliflower 5/8 oz / 200g. (yes)
Salt 1 pinch / 1g. (little)
Rice (whole grain) 1/2 cup / 60g. (yes)
Water 3 cups / 300g. (yes)
Salt 1 pinch / 1g. (little)

Cooking instructions:
Heat sesame oil in a hot pot. Add chopped onions, grated ginger, dried thyme, plenty of cumin and sauté gently. Add peeled red lentils, a strip of wakame, a little lemon juice, hot water and some dried buckthorn fruits. Simmer for 20 minutes until the lentils are cooked; add hot water as needed to make a pulp. Add sugar, some chili and salt. Add vinegar or lemon juice depending on your taste. Add chopped tomatoes as desired. Let it pass for a few minutes.
Cook in a small pot with 1 cup of water and a little salt the cauliflower 10 min. until soft.
Blanch in a small pot with 1 cup of water and salt the chard 3 min.
Boil the rice briefly, salt and 10 min. to let go. Serve everything with the lentil dish.

9.38 Fennel and potato gratin

Reduces inflammation, improves blood circulation, improves digestion, supports urination, lowers cholesterol, good to fight loss of appetite, flatulence, inflammatory bowel disease, heartburn. Forcing spleen, improves blood circulation.
Cooking time approx. 1 1/2 hours
Allergens: CGL
2 portions to 230,5g. / 147kcal. - (carb:68% / prot:32%)
100g.=63,77kcal. / protein 5,72g. fat:5,42g.
µg. - Ph:15 Na:12,98 Ka:80,91 Mg:13,52 Ca:40,41 Fe:0,41 Zn:0,09 Col.:7,81 Hsr.:3,64

Quantity of ingredients:
Fennel 5/8 oz / 200g. (yes)
Potato 1/4 lbs - 4oz / 125g. (yes)
Basic recipe for a vegetable soup (nutritious) 1/2 cup / 100g. (yes)
Butter organic 1 teaspoon / 3g. (little)
Rice flour 2 teaspoons / 6g. (yes)
Cream sour 10% 1 teaspoon / 3g. (yes)
Salt 1 pinch / 1g. (little)
Sugar cane sugar 1 pinch / 1g. (little)
Chicken yolk 1 piece / 10g. (yes)
Pepper Cayenne 1 pinch / 0,5g. (yes)
Nutmeg 1 pinch / 0,5g. (yes)
Parsley 1 teaspoon / 2g. (yes)
Chives 1 teaspoon / 3g. (yes)
Butter organic 1 teaspoon / 3g. (little)

Cooking instructions:
Cook peeled potatoes and then let cool. Wash the fennel, cut off the stems and remove any outer leaves.
Hold back fennel greens and add it to the sauce with the other herbs later.
Steam the fennel tubers for about 15 - 20 minutes.
Then cut the potatoes and fennel into slices and place in layers in a greased baking dish.
Bring the liquid of fennel broth to the boil and bind it with flour.
Season with sea salt, cayenne pepper, sugar, nutmeg and sour cream. Allow to cool and alloy with egg yolk.
Spread the sauce over the casserole, sprinkle with parmesan and finely chopped parsley and chives. Bake at 200 °C / 392 °F in the oven for half an hour.

9.39 Fish soup with rosemary

Promotes spleen and liver, reduces blood pressure, strengthens immune system, prevents cancer, reduces radiation damage, has little cholesterol and is protein rich, improves blood circulation, increases appetite. Antioxidant, forcing spleen, dissolves stagnation.
Cooking time approx. 30 min
Allergens: DLO
4 portions to 284,25g. / 271kcal. - (carb:38% / prot:62%)
100g.=95,43kcal. / protein 15,39g. fat:14,78g.
µg. - Ph:4,93 Na:1,8 Ka:11,89 Mg:0,76 Ca:1,33 Fe:0,03 Zn:0,03 Col.:0,01 Hsr.:3,59

Quantity of ingredients:
Basic recipe for a fish soup 2 cup / 500g. (yes)
Rosemary 1/2 bunch / 7g. (yes)
Onion (spring onion) 1 piece / 20g. (yes)
Olive oil 2 table spoons / 35g. (yes)
Fish pieces mixed (fresh water) 5/8 lbs - 8oz / 250g. (yes)
Carrot 1 piece / 120g. (yes)
Parsnip 1 piece / 180g. (yes)
Celery root 1 slice / 20g. (yes)
Salt 1 pinch / 1g. (little)
Peppercorns 2 pieces / 1g. (yes)
Garlic 1 clove / 3g. (yes)

Cooking instructions:
Fry the onion and garlic in oil. Add fish broth. Add diced carrots, parsnips and celery. Season with salt and peppercorns. Simmer the soup on a low heat for 25 minutes.

Wash the fish, drizzle with lemon juice, divide into pieces and add to the soup with the pink rosemary. Cook for 5 min on low heat.
Add the chives and parsley and season the soup with the salt.

9.40 Frozen pineapple juice

Pineapple reduce inflammation, supports urination, cleans the skin.
Cooking time approx. 1 1/2 hours
1 portion to 50g. / 29kcal. - (carb:95% / prot:5%)
100g.=58kcal. / protein 0,25g. fat:0,1g.
µg. - Ph:9 Na:2 Ka:173 Mg:17 Ca:16 Fe:0,4 Zn:0,3 Col.:0 Hsr.:7

Quantity of ingredients:
Pineapple 1/8 lbs - 2oz / 50g. (yes)

Cooking instructions:
Juice pineapple yourself or freeze the organic pineapple juice in small portions and if necessary suck.

9.41 Fruit juice

Stops diarrhea, promotes digestion, appetizing, harmonizes the stomach, relieves pain, detoxifying, reduces blood pressure, strengthens immune system, prevents cancer, reduces radiation damage.
Cooking time approx. 10 min
2 portions to 305g. / 176kcal. - (carb:93% / prot:7%)
100g.=57,54kcal. / protein 1,89g. fat:0,9g.
µg. - Ph:4,99 Na:2,24 Ka:37,45 Mg:2,36 Ca:6,04 Fe:0,21 Zn:0,05 Col.:0 Hsr.:4,3

Quantity of ingredients:
Orange 2 pieces / 150g. (yes)
Apple (sweet) 4 pieces / 300g. (yes)
Carrot 2 pieces / 150g. (yes)
Honey 1 table spoon / 10g. (little)

Cooking instructions:
Peel oranges and carrots. Cut all ingredients into cubes so that they fit into the juicer and juice. Sweet with honey.

9.42 Grated apple

Eat 3 times a day - Apple (sour) scraped and brown is stuffing. Relieves diarrhea.
Cooking time approx. 10 min
1 portion to 200g. / 120kcal. - (carb:94% / prot:6%)
100g.=60kcal. / protein 0,6g. fat:0,8g.
µg. - Ph:11 Na:3 Ka:144 Mg:6 Ca:7 Fe:0,5 Zn:0,1 Col.:0 Hsr.:15

Quantity of ingredients:
Apple (sour) 1 piece / 200g. (yes)

Cooking instructions:
Peel apple and grate as fine as possible. Leave for at least 5 minutes until it turns brown.

9.43 Grated carrots with apple

Promotes spleen and liver, reduces blood pressure, strengthens immune system, prevents cancer, reduces radiation damage, stops diarrhea, promotes digestion, appetizing, harmonizes the stomach.
Cooking time approx. 10 min
1 portion to 154g. / 74kcal. - (carb:91% / prot:9%)
100g.=48,05kcal. / protein 1,21g. fat:0,41g.
µg. - Ph:26,57 Na:19,84 Ka:140,47 Mg:10,21 Ca:29,74 Fe:1,4 Zn:0,36 Col.:0 Hsr.:18,25

Quantity of ingredients:
Carrot 1/4 lbs - 4oz / 100g. (yes)
Apple (sweet) 1 piece / 50g. (yes)
Lemon juice 2 teaspoons / 3g. (yes)
Sugar substitute (sweetener) 1g. Or 0,034oz / 1g. (yes)

Cooking instructions:
Mix lemon juice with sweetener. Grate the washed, thinly peeled carrots and the apple piece into the sauce and mix.

9.44 Halibut with tomato and garlic sauce

Promotes digestion, helps to digest fat, supports urination, reduces blood pressure, good to fight rheumatism, flatulence, bladder weakness, anemia, high blood pressure, depressions, diabetes, diarrhea. Valuable omega-3 fatty acids.
Cooking time approx. 45 min

Allergens: D
5 portions to 297,6g. / 319kcal. - (carb:36% / prot:64%)
100g.=107,19kcal. / protein 34,96g. fat:9,44g.
µg. - Ph:4,82 Na:8,78 Ka:7,08 Mg:1,03 Ca:0,88 Fe:0,02 Zn:0,01 Col.:0,82 Hsr.:4,78

Quantity of ingredients:
Rice variety any 1 cup / 120g. (yes)
Water 6 cups / 240g. (yes)
Salt 1 pinch / 1g. (little)
Halibut (Flatfish) 2,2 lbs / 800g. (yes)
Salt 1 pinch / 1g. (little)
Pepper (ground) 1 pinch / 0,5g. ()
Lemon juice 1 splash / 2g. (yes)
Bay leaf 2 pieces / 2g. (yes)
Lemon 1 piece / 30g. (yes)
Garlic 8 pieces / 10g. (yes)
Thyme dried 1 table spoon / 5g. (yes)
Olives 0,2 lbs / 75g. (yes)
Tomato 4 pieces / 200g. (yes)
Salt 1 pinch / 1g. (little)
Pepper (ground) 1 pinch / 0,5g. ()

Cooking instructions:
Cook rice with salted water (1:3).
Rinse the fish under running cold water, dab with kitchen paper and rub with salt, pepper and lemon juice.
Place the fish fillets in a casserole dish with pieces of bay leaf.

Wash the lemon hot and cut into slices, peel and halve the garlic.
Sprinkle the olives and the thyme over them.
Brew the tomatoes with hot water, skin and chop.

Mix all ingredients, season with salt and pepper and distribute around the fish.
Cook everything at 200°C/392°F for about 20 minutes.
Serve with the rice.

9.45 Hungarian rice salad

Promotes digestion, helps to digest fat, supports urination, reduces blood pressure, strengthens kidney and bladder, diuretic, warming the body from the inside, expands blood vessels, strengthens the muscles, regulates internal organs functions.
Cooking time approx. 25 min

Allergens: GM
2 portions to 323,5g. / 421kcal. - (carb:54% / prot:46%)
100g.=130,14kcal. / protein 8,23g. fat:14,84g.
µg. - Ph:18,97 Na:10,25 Ka:26,18 Mg:5,55 Ca:14,42 Fe:0,12 Zn:0,11 Col.:0,77 Hsr.:4,63

Quantity of ingredients:
Rice (whole grain) 1/2 cup / 60g. (yes)
Water 3 cups / 300g. (yes)
Salt 1 pinch / 0,3g. (little)
Tomato 1/4 lbs - 4oz / 100g. (yes)
Peppers 1/8 lbs - 2oz / 50g. (yes)
Champignon 1 oz / 30g. (yes)
Edam cheese 1 oz / 30g. (yes)
Yogurt (natural, 1.5% fat) 1/8 lbs - 2oz / 45g. (yes)
Salt 1 pinch / 1g. (little)
Rapeseed oil 2 table spoons / 20g. (yes)
Pepper (ground) 1 pinch / 0,2g. ()

Cooking instructions:
Pour the rice into plenty of boiling salt water and let it drain gently.
Wash tomatoes and peppers and core. Cut both in to small cubes. Peel
the mushrooms (from the tin or with rapeseed oil for a short time) and
cut the cheese into small cubes and add to the rice. Prepare the
marinade and mix with the ingredients, refrigerate and leave for at least
an hour.

9.46 Kohlrabi in chervil sauce with potatoes

Reduces inflammation, lowers cholesterol, diuretic, conducts bowel
winds, strengthens immune system, prevents cancer, promotes weight
loss. Good to fight loss of appetite, flatulence, high blood pressure,
depressions, diabetes, diarrhea.
Cooking time approx. 1 hour
Allergens: GL
4 portions to 316,75g. / 188kcal. - (carb:79% / prot:21%)
100g.=59,19kcal. / protein 8,66g. fat:2,51g.
µg. - Ph:2,95 Na:1,03 Ka:25,06 Mg:3,48 Ca:15,16 Fe:0,04 Zn:0,02 Col.:0,06 Hsr.:0,91

Quantity of ingredients:
Potato 6 pieces / 450g. (yes)
Basic recipe for a vegetable soup (nutritious) 1 cup / 300g. (yes)
Potato 1/4 lbs - 4oz / 100g. (yes)
Nutmeg 1 pinch / 0,2g. (yes)
Lemon peel 1/2 teaspoon / 2g. (yes)

Ginger fresh 1/2 teaspoon / 2g. (yes)
Lovage 1/2 teaspoon / 2g. (yes)
Kohlrabi 3/4 lbs / 300g. (yes)
Salt 1 pinch / 1g. (little)
Pepper (ground) 1 pinch / 0,2g. ()
Sour cream 15% fat 3 table spoons / 30g. (little)
Chervil dried 1 Bunch / 80g. (yes)

Cooking instructions:
Boil the potatoes in salted water.
Bring half of the vegetable stock to boil. Add the diced potatoes,
nutmeg, lemon zest, ginger and lovage. Cover the potatoes and cook
for about 10 minutes until soft and puree them with a blender until they
are smooth.
Bring remaining vegetable stock to boil. Cut kohlrabi into cubes and
add, cover and cook for about 8 minutes. Stir in the potato sauce and
heat everything briefly.
Puree with the mixing stick chervil and sour cream. Mix the chervil
cream with the kohlrabi vegetables.
Serve with the cooked, peeled potatoes.

9.47 Leek and potato gratin

Reduces inflammation, improves digestion, regenerates skin, supports
urination, lowers cholesterol, promotes sweating, dissolves stagnation.
Cooking time approx. 1 hour
Allergens: CGL
4 portions to 346,5g. / 368kcal. - (carb:56% / prot:44%)
100g.=106,35kcal. / protein 7,73g. fat:16,47g.
µg. - Ph:3,43 Na:5,61 Ka:14,59 Mg:1,08 Ca:3,84 Fe:0,04 Zn:0,03 Col.:1,24 Hsr.:1,42

Quantity of ingredients:
Potato 1,1 lbs / 500g. (yes)
Leek 1,1 lbs / 500g. (yes)
Apple (sour) 1 piece / 200g. (yes)
Crème fraiche cheese 1/4 lbs - 4oz / 125g. (little)
Basic recipe for a vegetable soup (nutritious) 1/4 cup / 20g. (yes)
Chicken yolk 1 piece / 20g. (yes)
Emmental cheese 2 table spoons / 20g. (yes)
Salt 1 pinch / 1g. (little)
Pepper (ground) 1 pinch / 0,5g. ()

Cooking instructions:
Wash the potatoes, peel, cut into very thin slices and pat dry. Place half in a flat greased baking dish.
Clean and wash leeks and cut into fine rings. Wash apple, peel and cut into thin slices. Spread the leek rings and apple slices on top. Put the remaining potato slices on top.
Mix crème fraîche, egg yolk, grated Emmentaler, salt and pepper, if necessary add some vegetable stock and pour over the casserole.
Bake at 200°C/392°F in the oven for about 45 to 50 minutes until golden brown. Cover with parchment paper after 30 minutes to prevent the burr from drying out.

9.48 Lentil and chestnut soup with curry

Reduces blood pressure, strengthens immune system, prevents cancer, reduces radiation damage, forcing spleen, dissolves stagnation, promotes weight loss. Good to fight immunodeficiency, loss of appetite, flatulence, high blood pressure, depressions, diabetes, diarrhea.
Cooking time approx. 45 min
Allergens: LO
4 portions to 238,25g. / 175kcal. - (carb:83% / prot:17%)
100g.=73,45kcal. / protein 4,17g. fat:4,33g.
µg. - Ph:2,67 Na:3,8 Ka:7,98 Mg:4,63 Ca:15,86 Fe:0,06 Zn:0,02 Col.:0 Hsr.:2,07

Quantity of ingredients:
Lentils red 3/8 lbs - 6oz / 150g. (yes)
Chestnuts 3/8 lbs - 6oz / 150g. (yes)
Olive oil 1 table spoon / 10g. (yes)
Curry 2 teaspoons / 8g. (yes)
Turmeric (yellow root) 1 teaspoon / 2g. (rec.)
Basic recipe for a vegetable soup (nutritious) 2 cup / 500g. (yes)
White wine 1/2 cup / 125g. (little)
Anise (Common Fennel) 1 pinch / 1g. (yes)
Cardamom 1 pinch / 0,5g. (yes)
Parsley 2 table spoons / 6g. (yes)

Cooking instructions:
Add the olive oil to a pan, sauté the chestnuts, sprinkle with the curry, add the lentils and season with vegetable stock, add a little white wine, mix in the curcuma, simmer for about 20 minutes (until the chestnuts are tender).
Then puree the soup.
Taste with a pinch of anise, cardamom and herbal salt. At the end, sprinkle finely chopped parsley over it.

9.49 Lettuce with vinegar dressing

Relieves fatigue, regulates gastrointestinal function, dissolves stagnation, laxative, antiparasitic, improves blood circulation, detoxifying, reduces inflammation, relieves pain.
Cooking time approx. 10 min
Allergens: O
2 portions to 127,5g. / 68kcal. - (carb:32% / prot:68%)
100g.=52,94kcal. / protein 1,64g. fat:4,88g.
µg. - Ph:8,07 Na:2,56 Ka:49,71 Mg:2,9 Ca:8,86 Fe:0,22 Zn:0,09 Col.:0 Hsr.:5

Quantity of ingredients:
Lettuce 1 piece / 200g. (rec.)
Vinegar (Apple vinegar) 1 table spoon / 10g. (yes)
Water 1 table spoon / 10g. (yes)
Rapeseed oil 1 table spoon / 10g. (yes)
Onion (spring onion) 1 piece / 20g. (yes)
Salt 1 pinch / 0,5g. (little)
Pepper (ground) 1 pinch / 0,1g. ()
Chives 1 table spoon / 5g. (yes)

Cooking instructions:
Clean lettuce, wash and drain. Add the ingredients to the marinade in an extra container. Salad with marinade just before consumption. Just before, sprinkle with chives.

9.50 Mango banana yoghurt drink ice cold

Good to fight loss of appetite, oral mucosa inflammation. Regulates gastrointestinal function, chronic constipation. Prevents cancer. Diuretic, forcing spleen.
Cooking time approx. 5 min
Allergens: G
2 portions to 226g. / 121kcal. - (carb:87% / prot:13%)
100g.=53,54kcal. / protein 2,72g. fat:1,05g.
µg. - Ph:7,97 Na:3,73 Ka:51,04 Mg:5,37 Ca:11,04 Fe:0,07 Zn:0,04 Col.:0,28 Hsr.:2,87

Quantity of ingredients:
Mango juice 1/2 cup / 100g. (little)
Yogurt (natural, 1.5% fat) 1/4 lbs - 4oz / 100g. (yes)
Banana 1/2 piece / 150g. (yes)
Acerola fruit nectar or powder 1 teaspoon / 2g. (little)

Cooking instructions:
Mix all the ingredients and 2-3 ice cubes in a blender.

9.51 Marinated cod on pumpkin puree

Reduces inflammation, improves digestion, promotes spleen, lung, stomach and kidneys, diuretic, reduces blood glucose, good to fight constipation and flatulence, dissolves stagnation.
Cooking time approx. 2 hours
Allergens: DG
4 portions to 288,5g. / 202kcal. - (carb:49% / prot:51%)
100g.=69,84kcal. / protein 17,24g. fat:5,13g.
µg. - Ph:5,4 Na:2,01 Ka:17,22 Mg:1,4 Ca:2,11 Fe:0,03 Zn:0,02 Col.:1,02 Hsr.:2,55

Quantity of ingredients:
Potato 6 pieces / 400g. (yes)
Pumpkin 5/8 oz / 200g. (yes)
Onion white 1 piece / 50g. (yes)
Oregano dried 1/2 teaspoon / 1g. (yes)
Lemon juice 1/2 piece / 15g. (yes)
Salt 1 pinch / 1g. (little)
Pepper (ground) 1 pinch / 0,3g. ()
Crème fraiche cheese 2 table spoons / 30g. (little)
Yogurt (natural, 1.5% fat) 3/8 lbs - 6oz / 150g. (yes)
Oregano dried 1/4 teaspoon / 1g. (yes)
Basil (fresh) 1/2 teaspoon / 2g. (yes)
Basil (fresh) 1/2 teaspoon / 2g. (yes)
Cod 3/4 lbs / 300g. (yes)
Salt 1 pinch / 1g. (little)
Pepper (ground) 1 pinch / 0,3g. ()
Olive oil 1 teaspoon / 3g. (yes)

Cooking instructions:
Mix yoghurt with oregano, basil and thyme. Wash the fish fillets, pat dry, place in a flat shape and pour over the marinade. Leave 2 hours in refrigerator.

Cook the potatoes in salted water until soft and peel.

Sauté the onion in oil until glassy, add the diced pumpkin and cook for about 10 min. Add oregano, lemon juice, salt, pepper and creme fraiche and puree with the blender.

Remove fish fillets from the marinade, drain, pat dry and salt. Coat a coated grill pan with 2 teaspoons of oil. Roast the fish fillets on both sides for 3 - 4 minutes and arrange with the potatoes on the pumpkin puree.

9.52 Noodle casserole with plugs and peaches

Relieves fatigue, relaxes, good to fight belching, acute or chronic obstruction of the bowel, flatulence, heartburn. Calms nerves and stomach, strengthens the defense, good to fight fungi infections.
Cooking time approx. 1 hour
Allergens: ACGO
4 portions to 293,5g. / 442kcal. - (carb:66% / prot:34%)
100g.=150,68kcal. / protein 17,55g. fat:19,06g.
µg. - Ph:6,51 Na:1,67 Ka:9,15 Mg:1,2 Ca:2,53 Fe:0,05 Zn:0,03 Col.:3,85 Hsr.:2,45

Quantity of ingredients:
Peaches 1,1 lbs / 500g. (yes)
Noodles (wheat, ribbon noodles) with egg 5/8 oz / 200g. (yes)
Chicken egg 2 pieces / 120g. (yes)
Sugar - icing sugar 1/8 lbs - 2oz / 40g. (little)
Vanilla sugar natural 3 package / 3g. (little)
Lemon peel 1/2 piece / 2g. (yes)
Cinnamon ground 1/4 teaspoon / 1g. (yes)
Curd cheese 20% 5/8 lbs - 8oz / 250g. (yes)
Butter organic 2 teaspoons / 8g. (little)
Strawberry jam 4 table spoons / 50g. (little)

Cooking instructions:
Preheat oven to 180°C/356°F.
Put Peaches briefly in boiling water, drain and peel off the skin. Cut peaches into small slices.
Cook noodles in plenty of salted water until firm, drain, chill off cold and drain.
Separate eggs. Stir egg yolks with icing sugar, vanilla sugar, grated lemon zest and cinnamon until fluffy with the whisk. Stir in the curd cheese. Add the noodles.
Beat the egg whites into firm snow and carefully lift them under the pasta.
Spread a baking dish thinly with butter. Alternating pate noodle mixture and peach slices into the form layers. Finish
with the pasta mixture. Sprinkle the casserole with butter flakes and bake in a preheated oven for 3o minutes.
Serve portion by portion with a tablespoon of jam.

9.53 Noodles with vegetable and tomato sauce

Protects the digestive system. Detoxifying, Good to fight loss of appetite, flatulence, inflammatory bowel disease, obesity, gout, stomach ulcers, stomach cramps, rheumatism, heartburn, twelffinger intestinal ulcers, promotes digestion, helps to digest fat.
Cooking time approx. 45 min
Allergens: ACG
2 portions to 281g. / 562kcal. - (carb:70% / prot:30%)
100g.=199,82kcal. / protein 14,06g. fat:21,68g.
µg. - Ph:21,13 Na:3,21 Ka:44,61 Mg:8,06 Ca:6,77 Fe:0,3 Zn:0,2 Col.:8,37 Hsr.:18,02

Quantity of ingredients:
Tomato 1/4 lbs - 4oz / 125g. (yes)
Carrot 1 piece / 80g. (yes)
Zucchini 1 piece / 80g. (yes)
Olive oil 1 table spoon / 15g. (yes)
Onion (shallot) 1 piece / 20g. (yes)
Oregano dried 1 pinch / 1g. (yes)
Salt 1 pinch / 1g. (little)
Pepper (ground) 1 pinch / 0,2g. ()
Noodles (wheat) with egg 5/8 oz / 200g. (yes)
Olive oil 1 table spoon / 10g. (yes)
Crème fraiche cheese 2 table spoons / 30g. (little)

Cooking instructions:
Boil the tomatoes with a little water, drain and collect the juice, cut the tomatoes into pieces.
Roughly grate zucchini and carrot. Heat olive oil in a pot. Steam shallots very soft. Add tomatoes, season with oregano, salt and pepper. Simmer tomatoes to a thick sauce.
Bring plenty of salted water to boil, cook the wholegrain noodles until firm. In the cooking time of the pasta, heat in a pan olive oil. Fry the carrots while stirring, lightly salt. Add zucchini, sauté
briefly while stirring. The vegetables should be soft with a bite.
Drain pasta, mix with crème fraiche, season with salt and pepper.
Garnish with the tomato sauce.

9.54 Oat flakes with aromatic spices

Stops diarrhea, promotes digestion, appetizing, harmonizes the stomach, relieves diarrhea, strengthens immune system, detoxifying and stimulating the immune system.
Cooking time approx. 25 min

Allergens: AH

3 portions to 208g. / 280kcal. - (carb:69% / prot:31%)
100g.=134,78kcal. / protein 6,73g. fat:10,72g.
µg. - Ph:11,3 Na:0,78 Ka:17,25 Mg:4,26 Ca:2,68 Fe:0,15 Zn:0,11 Col.:0 Hsr.:4,12

Quantity of ingredients:

Oat flakes (whole grain) 1 cup / 125g. (yes)
Walnuts 1 table spoon / 15g. (yes)
Hazelnuts 1 table spoon / 15g. (yes)
Water 1 1/2 cups / 240g. (yes)
Wakame 1 inch / 2g. (yes)
Apple (sweet) 1 piece / 220g. (yes)
Cardamom 3-4 capsules / 2g. (yes)
Lemon Balm (fresh) 3-4 leaves / 3g. (yes)
Acerola fruit nectar or powder 1 teaspoon / 2g. (little)

Cooking instructions:

Roast oatmeal and nuts. Add hot water. Add cardamom, wakame and cook for 20 min. Add grated apple, acerola and lemon herb.

9.55 Oriental rice pan

Forcing spleen, dissolves stagnation, promotes weight loss. Good to fight immunodeficiency, loss of appetite, flatulence, high blood pressure, helps to digest fat, strengthens kidney and bladder. Numerous vitamins, minerals and secondary plant active ingredients. Cooking time approx. 30 min

Allergens: EL

6 portions to 271,83g. / 303kcal. - (carb:81% / prot:19%)
100g.=111,47kcal. / protein 9,51g. fat:5,44g.
µg. - Ph:2,35 Na:0,71 Ka:4,97 Mg:1,97 Ca:4,24 Fe:0,03 Zn:0,01 Col.:0 Hsr.:2,04

Quantity of ingredients:

Rice (whole grain) 3/8 lbs - 6oz / 180g. (yes)
Basic recipe for a vegetable soup (nutritious) 2 1/4 cups / 500g. (yes)
Curry 1/2 teaspoon / 2g. (yes)
Onion (spring onion) 4 pieces / 80g. (yes)
Rapeseed oil 2 table spoons / 20g. (yes)
Peppers 1/4 lbs - 4oz / 120g. (yes)
Corn 3 oz / 80g. (yes)
Shiitake, dried 1/2 oz / 80g. (yes)
Bamboo shoots 3 oz / 80g. (yes)
Peas 3 oz / 80g. (yes)
Peaches 1/8 lbs - 2oz / 60g. (yes)

Pineapple 1/8 lbs - 2oz / 60g. (yes)
Tomato 5/8 oz / 200g. (yes)
Lovage 1 teaspoon / 2g. (yes)
Basil (fresh) 1 teaspoon / 2g. (yes)
Parsley 1 teaspoon / 2g. (yes)
Lemon Balm (fresh) 1 teaspoon / 2g. (yes)
Pepper (ground) 1 pinch / 1g. ()

Cooking instructions:
Soak the mushrooms in water 20 min.
Boil the rice in the vegetable stock 15 min. and season with some curry.
Peel the onion, cut into fine cubes.
Heat the oil in a pan and sauté the onion cubes.
Wash the peppers in half, remove the core, cut into cubes and add.
Add corn, mushrooms and bamboo shoots, simmer 5 min. until firm.
Also add the bean sprouts, peas, peach cubes and pineapple cubes.
Then add the peeled, chopped tomatoes.
Add the cooked rice and season with the herbs and pepper.

9.56 Pancakes with spinach and parmesan

Promotes bowel movement, improves blood circulation, forcing spleen
and bowel, strengthens immune system, good to fight loss of appetite,
flatulence, high blood pressure, depressions, diabetes, constipation,
inflammatory bowel disease
Cooking time approx. 25 min
Allergens: ACGL
6 portions to 303g. / 330kcal. - (carb:46% / prot:54%)
100g.=108,8kcal. / protein 17,5g. fat:18,52g.
µg. - Ph:3,27 Na:3,24 Ka:6,47 Mg:0,96 Ca:4,52 Fe:0,05 Zn:0,02 Col.:1,32 Hsr.:1,02

Quantity of ingredients:
Wheat flour 1/4 lbs - 4oz / 100g. (yes)
Chicken egg 4 pieces / 200g. (yes)
Cow's milk (whole milk 3.5% fat) 1 1/2 cups / 400g. (yes)
Salt 1 pinch / 1g. (little)
Sunflower oil 1 table spoon / 15g. (yes)
Olive oil 1 table spoon / 15g. (yes)
Onion white 1 piece / 50g. (yes)
Parsley 1/2 bunch / 80g. (yes)
Basic recipe for a vegetable soup (nutritious) 1/2 cup / 150g. (yes)
Basil (fresh) 1/4 teaspoon / 1g. (yes)

Basil (fresh) 1/4 teaspoon / 1g. (yes)
Nutmeg 1 pinch / 0,3g. (yes)
Crème fraiche cheese 3 table spoons / 45g. (little)
Spinach 1,3 lbs / 600g. (yes)
Salt 1 pinch / 1g. (little)
Pepper (ground) 1 pinch / 0,1g. ()

Cooking instructions:
Stir flour, eggs and milk and a pinch of salt with the whisk until smooth.
From the dough, fry pancakes crispy brown on both sides.

Heat oil in a small saucepan. Fry the finely chopped onion until tender.
Stir in chopped parsley, sauté briefly. Add the vegetable broth
according to the basic recipe, season with basil and nutmeg. Cover and
simmer for 15 minutes, add creme fraiche and finely puree.
Cook the washed, drizzled spinach with a little salt in a closed pan over
a moderate heat in 3 minutes, drain in a sieve and cut into small pieces.
Add the spinach to the sauce, heat briefly. Add parmesan in the mix.
Fill the pancakes with the cream spinach.

9.57 Plum Cake

Cancer preventive effect, dehydrates the body, stimulates digestion and
binds fats in the intestine, good to fight loss of appetite, flatulence,
inflammatory bowel disease, obesity, gout, stomach ulcers, stomach
cramps, rheumatism, heartburn. Relieves pain, detoxifying, bactericide.
Cooking time approx. 1 hour
Allergens: AG
6 portions to 307,83g. / 502kcal. - (carb:71% / prot:29%)
100g.=163,24kcal. / protein 12,32g. fat:19,28g.
µg. - Ph:2,65 Na:0,77 Ka:5,44 Mg:0,5 Ca:0,87 Fe:0,03 Zn:0,02 Col.:0,05 Hsr.:1,38

Quantity of ingredients:
Curd cheese 20% 5/8 oz / 200g. (yes)
Wheat flour 7/8 lbs / 400g. (yes)
Cow's milk (whole milk 3.5% fat) 6 table spoons / 70g. (yes)
Rapeseed oil 6 table spoons / 70g. (yes)
Honey 8 table spoons / 100g. (little)
Salt 1 pinch / 1g. (little)
Cinnamon ground 1 teaspoon / 3g. (yes)
Plums 2,2 lbs / 1000g. (yes)

Cooking instructions:
Mix the flour, curd cheese, milk, oil, honey, salt and baking powder into a smooth dough. Keep the dough cool for 15 minutes to cool.
Lay out baking paper on a baking sheet and press the dough out to a bottom.
Now spread the plums evenly.
Sprinkle the cake with the cinnamon and bake for about 40 minutes at 190 ° C/374 °F.

9.58 Potato cream with herbs and fresh cheese

Good to fight loss of appetite, constipation, bloating and nausea. Improves digestion, supports urination, prevents cancer, forcing spleen, dissolves stagnation, relaxing and reassuring.
Cooking time approx. 25 min
Allergens: G
2 portions to 218,5g. / 217kcal. - (carb:14% / prot:86%)
100g.=99,31kcal. / protein 8,76g. fat:11,22g.
µg. - Ph:18,66 Na:18,04 Ka:73,64 Mg:4,87 Ca:13,9 Fe:0,13 Zn:0,09 Col.:4,84 Hsr.:2,24

Quantity of ingredients:
Potato (mealy) 5/8 lbs - 8oz / 250g. (yes)
Fresh cheese 3 oz / 80g. (yes)
Yogurt (natural, 1.5% fat) 3 table spoons / 45g. (yes)
Chives 1/2 bunch / 50g. (yes)
Basil (fresh) 1 teaspoon / 4g. (yes)
Parsley 1 teaspoon / 4g. (yes)
Dill 1/2 teaspoon / 2g. (yes)
Salt 1 pinch / 1g. (little)
Black caraway 1 pinch / 0,5g. (yes)
Pepper (ground) 1 pinch / 0,5g. ()

Cooking instructions:
Softly steam the potatoes in the pan, peel them and press through the potato press.
Mix cream cheese, yoghurt and herbs under the potatoes, season with salt, crushed black cumin and pepper.

9.59 Potato gnocchi with vegetables and basil sauce

Strengthens immune system, promotes weight loss. Good to fight immunodeficiency, loss of appetite, flatulence, high blood pressure. Relaxing and reassuring.
Cooking time approx. 1 hour
Allergens: ACGL
4 portions to 290,25g. / 167kcal. - (carb:75% / prot:25%)
100g.=57,45kcal. / protein 6,54g. fat:4,63g.
µg. - Ph:3,26 Na:1,11 Ka:13,57 Mg:2,45 Ca:9,39 Fe:0,06 Zn:0,02 Col.:1,36 Hsr.:1,49

Quantity of ingredients:
Potato 5/8 lbs - 8oz / 250g. (yes)
Wheat flour 1 oz / 25g. (yes)
Wheat semolina 1/2 oz / 15g. (yes)
Chicken yolk 1 piece / 20g. (yes)
Nutmeg 1 pinch / 0,2g. (yes)
Basic recipe for a vegetable soup (nutritious) 1 cup / 250g. (yes)
Celery root 1/8 lbs - 2oz / 50g. (yes)
Lemon peel 1/2 teaspoon / 2g. (yes)
Ginger fresh 1/2 teaspoon / 2g. (yes)
Nutmeg 1 pinch / 0,2g. (yes)
Basil (fresh) 1 Bunch / 125g. (yes)
Crème fraiche cheese 1 table spoon / 20g. (little)
Salt 1 pinch / 1g. (little)
Pepper (ground) 1 pinch / 0,2g. ()
Carrot 1/4 lbs - 4oz / 100g. (yes)
Zucchini 1/4 lbs - 4oz / 100g. (yes)
Cauliflower 1/4 lbs - 4oz / 100g. (yes)
Broccoli 1/4 lbs - 4oz / 100g. (yes)
Salt 1 pinch / 1g. (little)

Cooking instructions:
Steam the potatoes gently, peel and pass hot through the potato press. Process the hot potatoes with flour, semolina, egg, nutmeg and salt to a smooth dough. Let dough rest for 3o minutes.
Make small rolls (2 cm) out of the dough with flour-dusted hands, cut off 1 cm thin slices. To create the typical gnocchi shape, gently dab the dough pieces with your thumb. Leave the gnocchi in lightly boiling salted water for 6 - 8 minutes. Lift the gnocchi out of the pot with the skimmer.

Heat the vegetable stock till it boils. Add diced celery, grated lemon peel, finely chopped ginger and 1 pinch of nutmeg. Cover and simmer

for about 10 minutes. Using the blender, puree the vegetable broth, celery, chopped basil and crème fraiche into a smooth sauce. Season with salt and nutmeg.
Cut carrots, zucchini, cauliflower and broccoli into small pieces and cook covered in a sieve over steam for 8 minutes until firm.
Heat the sauce again and add to the vegetables and arrange over the gnocchi.

9.60 Potato-basil soup

Reduces inflammation, improves digestion, supports urination, lowers cholesterol, reduces blood pressure, strengthens immune system, prevents cancer, reduces radiation damage, antioxidative, dissolves stagnation.
Cooking time approx. 25 min
Allergens: L
4 portions to 330g. / 96kcal. - (carb:69% / prot:31%)
100g.=28,94kcal. / protein 3,23g. fat:2,99g.
µg. - Ph:1,91 Na:3,35 Ka:13,03 Mg:0,61 Ca:2,91 Fe:0,03 Zn:0,01 Col.:0 Hsr.:1,9

Quantity of ingredients:
Water 2 cups / 450g. (yes)
Potato 4 pieces / 200g. (yes)
Carrot 2 pieces / 100g. (yes)
Celery root 1 piece / 500g. (yes)
Pepper (ground) 1 pinch / 0,5g. ()
Ground 1 pinch / 1g. (yes)
Garlic 1 clove / 3g. (yes)
Salt 1 pinch / 1g. (little)
Lemon 1 teaspoon / 3g. (yes)
Basil (fresh) 1 Bunch / 50g. (yes)
Sugar cane sugar 1 pinch / 1g. (little)
Olive oil 1 table spoon / 10g. (yes)

Cooking instructions:
Peeled and chopped 4 medium potatoes in a pot of hot water and 2 chopped medium carrots, a piece of celery root, a pinch of pepper, a pinch of ground cumin, crushed a small clove of garlic, a pinch of salt, 1 teaspoon of lemon juice, simmer until the Vegetables Is soft.
Add 1 bunch finely chopped basil into one half of the soup and puree everything; stir in the other half of the basil; with rose paprika, a pinch of whole cane sugar, 1 tablespoon of olive oil or butter, freshly ground pepper, salt to taste.

9.61 Pumpkin-yoghurt soup

Relaxes, reduces blood pressure, strengthens immune system, promotes weight loss. Good to fight immunodeficiency, loss of appetite, flatulence, depressions, diabetes, diarrhea.
Cooking time approx. 15 min
Allergens: GL
4 portions to 239g. / 68kcal. - (carb:83% / prot:17%)
100g.=28,45kcal. / protein 2,37g. fat:1,31g.
µg. - Ph:1,79 Na:0,9 Ka:6,6 Mg:2,8 Ca:10,96 Fe:0,02 Zn:0,01 Col.:0,05 Hsr.:0,35

Quantity of ingredients:
Basic recipe for a vegetable soup (nutritious) 1 cup / 300g. (yes)
Hokkaido pumpkin 1,1 lbs / 500g. (yes)
Ginger fresh 1/2 teaspoon / 2g. (yes)
Anise (Common Fennel) 1/4 teaspoon / 1g. (yes)
Yogurt (natural, 1.5% fat) 3/8 lbs - 6oz / 150g. (yes)
Peppermint 2 leaves / 1g. (yes)
Salt 1 pinch / 1g. (little)

Cooking instructions:
Heat the vegetable broth (after the basic recipe) till it boils. Add diced pumpkin, chopped ginger, crushed fennel seeds and anise. Bring the soup to the boil and simmer for about 12 minutes until the pumpkin is soft. Remove soup from the heat. Puree the soup with the yoghurt with the blender. Serve soup with finely chopped mint sprinkled.

9.62 Quick zucchini soup

Diuretic, supports urination. Strengthens gastrointestinal function, expands blood vessels, prevents cancer, prevents diseases (in the elderly). Stimulates liver function, detoxifying.
Cooking time approx. 10 min
4 portions to 241,5g. / 42kcal. - (carb:46% / prot:54%)
100g.=17,29kcal. / protein 1,76g. fat:2,04g.
µg. - Ph:3,81 Na:0,41 Ka:29,78 Mg:3,2 Ca:5,37 Fe:0,21 Zn:0,01 Col.:0 Hsr.:2,85

Quantity of ingredients:
Zucchini 2-3 pieces / 500g. (yes)
Onion white 1 piece / 50g. (yes)
Corn germ oil 2 table spoons / 6g. (yes)
Parsley 1 table spoon / 7g. (yes)
Chives 1 teaspoon / 3g. (yes)
Water 2 cup / 400g. (yes)

Cooking instructions:
Fry chopped onion in oil. Add sliced zucchini and sauté well. Pour with water. Chop parsley and chives, add and puree everything.

9.63 Rhubarb and apple jelly

Antioxidants, lots of vitamin C, laxative, relieves pain, detoxifying, warms stomach and spleen, improves blood circulation.
Cooking time approx. 15 min
2 portions to 276,5g. / 180kcal. - (carb:96% / prot:4%)
100g.=65,1kcal. / protein 1,19g. fat:0,58g.
µg. - Ph:14,75 Na:1,5 Ka:93,5 Mg:7,42 Ca:12,73 Fe:0,29 Zn:0,07 Col.:0 Hsr.:6,21

Quantity of ingredients:
Rhubarb 5/8 oz / 200g. (yes)
Apple juice (natural cloudy) 1 cup / 300g. (little)
Corn starch 1 oz / 30g. (yes)
Honey 1/2 oz / 20g. (little)
Vanilla sugar natural 1 pinch / 0,5g. (little)
Cinnamon ground 1 pinch / 0,5g. (yes)
Peppermint 2 leaves / 2g. (yes)

Cooking instructions:
Add the cornstarch to a 1/2 cup apple juice.
Simmer the rhubarb in 1 cup of water for 10 min.
Add the remaining apple juice and the cornstarch, stir, heat till it boils again.
Sweet with honey and season with vanilla and cinnamon. Spread the mixture on dessert bowls and garnish with mint.

9.64 Rice congee with honey pear and black sesame

Promotes digestion, supports urination, good to fight blood circulation disorders, thromboses, risk of embolism, high blood pressure, a headache, heart attack and stroke.
Cooking time approx. 10 min - 3 hours
Allergens: N
2 portions to 271,5g. / 158kcal. - (carb:95% / prot:5%)
100g.=58,38kcal. / protein 2,43g. fat:1,55g.
µg. - Ph:4,8 Na:0,43 Ka:18,44 Mg:35,15 Ca:34,31 Fe:0,09 Zn:0,06 Col.:0 Hsr.:2,88

Quantity of ingredients:
Basic recipe for a rice soup (Congee) 1 1/2 cups / 240g. (yes)
Pear 2 pieces / 300g. (yes)

Cooking instructions:
Cook rice congee according to basic recipe.
Fill pot with 3 cm of water and heat till it boils. Quarter the pears (with the skin and seeds) and simmer them covered with black sesame for 10 minutes. Mix with the rice.

9.65 Ricepudding

Regulates gastrointestinal function. Strengthens spleen and stomach, strengthens the muscles. Vitamin C rich.
Cooking time approx. 2 hours and more
Allergens: G
1 portion to 329g. / 316kcal. - (carb:76% / prot:24%)
100g.=96,05kcal. / protein 9,26g. fat:7,35g.
µg. - Ph:91,08 Na:31,47 Ka:222,68 Mg:30,22 Ca:77,57 Fe:0,44 Zn:0,42 Col.:3,65
Hsr.:17,51

Quantity of ingredients:
Cow's milk (whole milk 3.5% fat) 3/4 cup - 6 oz / 200g. (yes)
Rice round grain 1 oz / 25g. (yes)
Banana 1/4 lbs - 4oz / 100g. (yes)
Red berry (without sugar) 2 teaspoons / 4g. (yes)

Cooking instructions:
Heat half of the milk till it boils in a small saucepan.
Sprinkle the rice and cook on low heat for about 15 minutes.
Peel the banana, finely grate with the blender and add the beetroot juice.
Mix the banana bran under the hot rice.
Pour a pudding mold (about 1/4 liter of contents) in cold water.
Fill the banana rice in the mold and let the pudding swell at room temperature.
After about 3 hours it is solid and can be toppled.
Take the remaining milk as a drink.

9.66 Roasted barley patties

Improves digestion, lowers cholesterol, good to fight diarrhea, ulceration, joint pain, stomach problems. Promotes spleen and liver, reduces blood pressure, strengthens immune system, prevents cancer, reduces radiation damage, stimulates liver function.
Cooking time approx. 1 1/2 hours
Allergens: ACN
3 portions to 292,67g. / 398kcal. - (carb:63% / prot:37%)
100g.=135,99kcal. / protein 8,38g. fat:19,69g.
µg. - Ph:7,07 Na:4,18 Ka:17,24 Mg:2,02 Ca:2,5 Fe:0,08 Zn:0,04 Col.:2,76 Hsr.:2,93

Quantity of ingredients:
Water 1 1/2 cups / 250g. (yes)
Barley grouts 1 cup / 120g. (yes)
Potato 1 piece / 140g. (yes)
Carrot 1 piece / 120g. (yes)
Champignon 2-3 pieces / 25g. (yes)
Chicken egg 1 piece / 55g. (yes)
Onion white 1 piece / 50g. (yes)
Ginger fresh 1/2 teaspoon / 1g. (yes)
Pepper (ground) 1 pinch / 0,5g. ()
Salt 1 pinch / 1g. (little)
Lemon 1/2 piece / 15g. (yes)
Parsley 2 table spoons / 15g. (yes)
Sesame oil 2 table spoons / 50g. (yes)
Bread roll 1 piece / 35g. (little)

Cooking instructions:
Preparation:
Place 2 large cups of hot water in a saucepan; add 1 large cup of barley porridge; simmer for 2 minutes while stirring; then let it swell for 20 minutes on the switched off stove; take down and let cool.
Cook in boiling water 1 large potato, chopped and cut.
Soak 1 roll in hot water and squeeze well.
Then: Mix the barley groats and crushed the potato. Add 1 grated carrot, 2 - 3 chopped mushrooms, 1 egg, 1 finely chopped onion, 1/2 teaspoon grated ginger, a pinch of pepper, a pinch of salt, a little lemon juice, chopped parsley, plenty of rose paprika; knead well and form patties; heat sesame oil in a hot pan; fry the patties for about 15 minutes over a gentle heat; turn at half time.

Also fits well: lettuce, soybean vegetables.

9.67 Roasted millet with plum compote

Supports urination, promotes spleen and kidney, strengthens the defense. Good to fight fungi infections.
Cooking time approx. 30 min
4 portions to 218,25g. / 139kcal. - (carb:85% / prot:15%)
100g.=63,8kcal. / protein 3,57g. fat:1,24g.
µg. - Ph:2,99 Na:0,1 Ka:4,37 Mg:1,68 Ca:0,78 Fe:0,09 Zn:0,03 Col.:0 Hsr.:0,93

Quantity of ingredients:
Millet 1 cup / 120g. (yes)
Water 1 1/2 cups / 250g. (yes)
Plum 1 1/2 cups / 250g. (yes)
Vanilla pod 1 pinch / 1g. (yes)
Water 5/8 lbs - 8oz / 250g. (yes)
Cinnamon ground 1 pinch / 1g. (yes)
Acerola fruit nectar or powder 1/2 teaspoon / 1g. (little)

Cooking instructions:
Roast millet briefly, pour over water, heat till it boils and let stand for 20 min. to swell.

Cook plums with water, vanilla and cinnamon 10 min. then strain. Add acerola and add to the millet.

9.68 Rosemary Potatoes

Reduces Inflammation, improves digestion, regenerates skin, supports urination, lowers cholesterol. Rosemary stimulates digestion, strengthens lung, promotes spleen and kidney, dries out.
Cooking time approx. 30 min
2 portions to 216,5g. / 188kcal. - (carb:76% / prot:24%)
100g.=87,07kcal. / protein 4,21g. fat:5,25g.
µg. - Ph:11,51 Na:0,72 Ka:82,88 Mg:4,72 Ca:1,86 Fe:0,1 Zn:0,07 Col.:0 Hsr.:3,64

Quantity of ingredients:
Potato 6-8 pieces / 420g. (yes)
Olive oil 1 table spoon / 10g. (yes)
Rosemary 1 teaspoon / 2g. (yes)

Cooking instructions:
Cut the potatoes into half´s, apply a little olive oil on the cut surface, then salt, sprinkle 2 - 3 rosemary needles on the potatoes.
Place the potatoes on the baking tray and bake them in the preheated oven for approx. 25 minutes to 190°C/374°F.

9.69 Semolina dumpling soup

Reduces blood pressure, strengthens immune system, dissolves stagnation, promotes weight loss. Good to fight immunodeficiency, loss of appetite, flatulence, high blood pressure, diabetes, diarrhea.
Cooking time approx. 1 hour
Allergens: ACGLO
3 portions to 235,67g. / 287kcal. - (carb:74% / prot:26%)
100g.=121,78kcal. / protein 12,68g. fat:16,24g.
µg. - Ph:7,29 Na:3,79 Ka:6,29 Mg:7,72 Ca:17,64 Fe:0,11 Zn:0,11 Col.:5,65 Hsr.:2,66

Quantity of ingredients:
Butter organic 1/8 lbs - 2oz / 40g. (little)
Chicken egg 1 piece / 65g. (yes)
Salt 1 pinch / 1g. (little)
Pepper (ground) 1 pinch / 0,5g. ()
Nutmeg 1 pinch / 1g. (yes)
Wheat semolina 3 oz / 80g. (yes)
Basic recipe for a beef soup (warming) 2 cup / 500g. (yes)
Parsley 1 table spoon / 10g. (yes)
Chives 1 table spoon / 10g. (yes)

Cooking instructions:
Knead the ingredients for the dumplings to a firm dough and allow to swell for 30 minutes. Heat the broth (basic recipe for a beef broth warming). Then cut out with a spoon dumplings, place in the prepared broth and let stand for 20 minutes. Before serving, chop parsley and sprinkle with thinly sliced chives.

9.70 Semolina porridge with banana

Regulates gastrointestinal function, reduces inflammation, antiallergic, good to fight blood circulation disorders.
Cooking time approx. 15 min
Allergens: AG
1 portion to 284g. / 307kcal. - (carb:66% / prot:34%)
100g.=108,1kcal. / protein 10,57g. fat:10,72g.
µg. - Ph:116,7 Na:93,56 Ka:218,89 Mg:28,56 Ca:92,08 Fe:0,64 Zn:0,36 Col.:7,61
Hsr.:12,85

Quantity of ingredients:
Cow's milk (whole milk 3.5% fat) 3/4 cup - 6 oz / 200g. (yes)
Spelled semolina 3 table spoons / 30g. (yes)
Butter organic 1 teaspoon / 4g. (little)
Banana 1/2 piece / 50g. (yes)

Cooking instructions:
Heat the half of the milk in a small pot. Add the semolina and boil it shortly in the milk. Let it swell at low heat for 3 minutes with constant stirring. Remove the pot from the heat, add the remaining milk with the snow bean and place the mush in a small bowl. Add the butter and the battered banana.
For adults, a pinch of cinnamon can be spread over it.

9.71 Sliced chicken with walnuts and sherry

Strengthens blood, strengthens bone marrow, strengthens gastrointestinal function, expands blood vessels, prevents cancer, promotes perspiration, reduces blood lipids, stimulates.
Cooking time approx. 25 min
Allergens: EGHN
4 portions to 272g. / 304kcal. - (carb:36% / prot:64%)
100g.=111,76kcal. / protein 20,6g. fat:25,03g.
µg. - Ph:27,64 Na:7,43 Ka:30,23 Mg:7,29 Ca:3,8 Fe:0,28 Zn:0,02 Col.:1,77 Hsr.:19,84

Quantity of ingredients:
Butter organic 2 table spoons / 35g. (little)
Walnuts 2 table spoons / 25g. (yes)
Ginger fresh 1/2 teaspoon / 2g. (yes)
Onion (shallot) 2 pieces / 40g. (yes)
Salt 1 pinch / 1g. (little)
Chicken meat 3/4 lbs / 300g. (yes)
Sesame, white 1 teaspoon / 2g. (yes)
Black fungus mushroom 4 pieces / 3g. (yes)
Shiitake, dried 4 pieces / 5g. (yes)
Soy sauce 1 dash / 3g. (yes)
Rice (whole grain) 1 cup / 120g. (yes)
Water 6 cups / 550g. (yes)
Salt 1 pinch / 1g. (little)

Cooking instructions:
Heat butter or sesame oil in a hot pan; Sauté walnuts, copious grated ginger, chopped shallots or onions; Add the salt and the sliced chicken and sauté everything; Rose paprika, roasted sesame, soaked black fungus, shiitake mushrooms or mushrooms; with a shot sherry; infuse with water; Simmer for 5 to 10 minutes until the meat is cooked; Season with soy sauce.
Place the rice in salted water, heat till it boils and let it simmer over low heat for about 15 minutes. This fits: lamb's lettuce, Radicchio

9.72 Spring salad

Blood-forming, blood detoxifying, diuretic, good to fight stomach discomfort, improves digestion, diarrhea, helps to digest fat, supports urination, reduces blood pressure, detoxifying, reduces inflammation, diuretic.
Cooking time approx. 10 min
Allergens: AEMNO
4 portions to 214,25g. / 180kcal. - (carb:64% / prot:36%)
100g.=84,13kcal. / protein 7,68g. fat:5,56g.
µg. - Ph:14,38 Na:19,94 Ka:78,76 Mg:7,01 Ca:20,61 Fe:0,72 Zn:0,03 Col.:0 Hsr.:7,87

Quantity of ingredients:
Sorrel 3/8 lbs - 6oz / 150g. (yes)
Dandelion (young plants) 1/4 lbs - 4oz / 100g. (yes)
Mung bean sprouting 0,2 lbs / 75g. (yes)
Cress 1/4 lbs - 4oz / 100g. (yes)
Chives 1 Bunch / 50g. (yes)
Tomato 2 pieces / 100g. (yes)
Parsley 1 Bunch / 50g. (yes)
Soy sauce 1 dash / 3g. (yes)
White bread (wheat bread) 6 slices / 120g. (little)
Vinegar Aceto Balsamico / 8g. (yes)
Olive oil / 8g. (yes)

Cooking instructions:
Wash all salad´s, mix and prepare the sauce as follows:
Mix tahini with mustard and balsamic vinegar, tamari, olive oil, chives and half of parsley. Pour the sauce over the salad and sprinkle the remaining parsley just before serving.
Serve with the white bread.

9.73 Szeged fishbowl

Promotes spleen, stomach and kidneys, improves digestion, dissolves stagnation, reduces blood pressure, strengthens immune system.
Cooking time approx. 30 min
Allergens: ADL
2 portions to 380,5g. / 280kcal. - (carb:58% / prot:42%)
100g.=73,59kcal. / protein 25,32g. fat:3,09g.
µg. - Ph:25,89 Na:22,72 Ka:60,47 Mg:11,78 Ca:30,28 Fe:0,18 Zn:0,12 Col.:4,99 Hsr.:13,6

Quantity of ingredients:
Cod 5/8 oz / 200g. (yes)
Lemon 1/4 piece / 5g. (yes)
Pork Bacon 1/8 lbs - 2oz / 40g. (yes)
Onion (spring onion) 2 pieces / 40g. (yes)
Sauerkraut (cutted cabbage fermented) 5/8 lbs - 8oz / 250g. (yes)
Tomato paste 2 table spoons / 20g. (yes)
Basic recipe for a vegetable soup (nutritious) 1/2 cup / 150g. (yes)
Salt 1 pinch / 1g. (little)
Pepper (ground) 1 pinch / 0,5g. ()
Spelled wholemeal flour 1 teaspoon / 3g. (yes)

Cooking instructions:
Clean the fish fillets, sprinkle with lemon, salt.
Roast the bacon in a deep, large pan. Add the finely chopped onions
and roast for a short time. Add sauerkraut and tomato paste. Fill with
vegetable stock and stew for about 10 to 15 minutes with the lid closed.
Put prepared fish cubes on the sauerkraut. Season with paprika,
caraway, pepper and simmer for about 10 minutes over low heat.
Tie with some flour or cornstarch.
Serve with bread.

9.74 Tea from ginger with honey

Honey relieves pain, detoxifying, bactericide.
Fresh ginger encourages digestion, detoxifying, strengthens bodily
production, promotes perspiration, reduces blood lipids, stimulates,
dissolves stagnation.
Cooking time approx. 30 min
4 portions to 127,25g. / 5kcal. - (carb:98% / prot:2%)
100g.=3,73kcal. / protein 0,01g. fat:0g.
µg. - Ph:0,02 Na:0,07 Ka:0,17 Mg:0,08 Ca:0,32 Fe:0 Zn:0,01 Col.:0 Hsr.:0

Quantity of ingredients:
Ginger fresh 1 teaspoon / 3g. (yes)
Water 2 cup / 500g. (yes)
Honey 2 teaspoons / 6g. (little)

Cooking instructions:
Heat the water till it boils and put it aside. Add ginger and 20-30 min. to
let go. Sweet to taste with honey.

9.75 Tea Green tea

Green tea promotes digestion, supports urination, dissolves mucus, detoxifying, stimulates nerves, reduces blood lipids, lowers cholesterol, reduces inflammation.
Cooking time approx. 10 min
1 portion to 122g. / 2kcal. - (carb:20% / prot:80%)
100g.=1,64kcal. / protein 0g. fat:0g.
µg. - Ph:5,61 Na:1,07 Ka:27,59 Mg:4,07 Ca:9,43 Fe:0,03 Zn:0,1 Col.:0 Hsr.:0

Quantity of ingredients:
Green tea 1 teaspoon / 2g. (yes)
Water 1 cup / 120g. (yes)

Cooking instructions:
For each cup you use a teaspoonful or a teabag.
Pour green tea only with 60 to 80 ° C / 140 to 176 °F hot water, otherwise it will be bitter.
If the tea has a stimulating effect, let it draw for two to three minutes. It has a calming effect for a duration of five minutes (no longer, otherwise it will be bitter!).
Another method: Pour the tea leaves with about 70 ° C / 158 °F hot water and pour the water immediately again. Then just pour hot water again. The bitter substances disappear and the tea gets a milder aroma.

9.76 Tea mixture against general exhaustion

Good to fight general exhaustion. Antibacterial, encouragingly, good to fight loss of appetite, flatulence, heartburn.
Cooking time approx. 10 min
4 portions to 127g. / 2kcal. - (carb:55% / prot:45%)
100g.=1,57kcal. / protein 0,17g. fat:0,04g.
µg. - Ph:0,11 Na:0,11 Ka:0,93 Mg:0,13 Ca:0,63 Fe:0 Zn:0,01 Col.:0 Hsr.:0

Quantity of ingredients:
Lemon Balm (dried) 2 teaspoons / 3g. (yes)
Blackberry leaves 2 teaspoons / 3g. (yes)
Lavender blossoms 1 teaspoon / 2g. (yes)
Water 1 1/2 cups / 500g. (yes)

Cooking instructions:
Heat the water till it boils and put it aside. Add 2 g lemon balm, 2 g blackberry leaves, 1,5g lavender flowers, leave to stand covered for 10 minutes, then strain. Drink a cup three times a day.

9.77 Tea rooibos

Antioxidant, anti-inflammatory, anticancer, flavonoids, it also has a positive effect on Alzheimer, arteriosclerosis. Antiallergic, inhibits histamine release. Antibacterial, antiviral, antifungal, detoxifying (alkaline).
Cooking time approx. 10 min.
5 portions to 200,8g. / 0kcal. - (carb:0% / prot:0%)
100g.=0kcal. / protein 0g. fat:0g.
µg. - Ph:0 Na:0,04 Ka:0 Mg:0,04 Ca:0,2 Fe:0 Zn:0 Col.:0 Hsr.:0

Quantity of ingredients:
Water 4 cup / 1000g. (yes)

Cooking instructions:
Brew 3-4 teaspoons of rooibos with one liter of boiling water and leave for 6-10 minutes. With soft water you use less tea for the preparation, with harder water we recommend a higher dosage.

9.78 Thick pea soup

Supports urination, detoxifying, dissolves stagnation, improves blood circulation, strengthens liver and kidney, strengthens immune system.
Cooking time approx. 2-3 hours
Allergens: AN
3 portions to 255g. / 123kcal. - (carb:47% / prot:53%)
100g.=48,37kcal. / protein 4,36g. fat:7,3g.
µg. - Ph:3,44 Na:0,25 Ka:7,5 Mg:1,22 Ca:1,55 Fe:0,06 Zn:0,04 Col.:0 Hsr.:5,21

Quantity of ingredients:
Peas, green 3/8 lbs - 6oz / 150g. (yes)
Water 2 1/4 cups / 550g. (yes)
Sesame oil 1 table spoon / 20g. (yes)
Onion white 1/2 piece / 25g. (yes)
Ginger fresh 1/2 teaspoon / 1g. (yes)
Ground 1/2 teaspoon / 1g. (yes)
Oat meal 1 table spoon / 15g. (yes)
Salt 1 pinch / 1g. (little)
Parsley 1 stem / 2g. (yes)

Cooking instructions:
Soak dried peas before cooking. Sauté sesame oil, onion, a little oatmeal, ginger and cumin in a hot pot; add the peas and simmer for 2-3 hours; add salt at the end and purée with a blender; garnish with parsley.

9.79 Tomato soup

Promotes digestion, helps to digest fat, reduces blood pressure, dissolves stagnation. Contains unsaturated fatty acids, is antioxidative.
Cooking time approx. 10 min
2 portions to 290g. / 100kcal. - (carb:42% / prot:58%)
100g.=34,66kcal. / protein 1,78g. fat:7,9g.
µg. - Ph:4,2 Na:1,2 Ka:31,36 Mg:1,99 Ca:3,85 Fe:0,07 Zn:0,04 Col.:0,01 Hsr.:1,47

Quantity of ingredients:
Olive oil 1 table spoon / 15g. (yes)
Onion white 1 piece / 60g. (yes)
Cinnamon ground 1 pinch / 1g. (yes)
Basil (fresh) 1 teaspoon / 2g. (yes)
Basil (fresh) 1 teaspoon / 2g. (yes)
Pepper (ground) 1 pinch / 0,5g. ()
Salt 1 pinch / 1g. (little)
Tomato 6 pieces / 250g. (yes)
Water 5/8 lbs - 8oz / 250g. (yes)

Cooking instructions:
Roast the onion in a pot. Salt and spices. Briefly roast. Put washed and quartered tomatoes in the pan. Stir and sauté briefly. Add a quart of water and heat till it boils. Cook for a quarter of an hour and puree.

9.80 Tomato with mozzarella

Promotes digestion, helps to digest fat, supports urination, reduces blood pressure. Affects anorexia, good to fight flatulence, inflammatory bowel disease, bloating and nausea. Relaxing and reassuring.
Cooking time approx. 5 min
Allergens: AG
1 portion to 217g. / 436kcal. - (carb:37% / prot:63%)
100g.=200,92kcal. / protein 14,85g. fat:30,31g.
µg. - Ph:90,53 Na:176,32 Ka:158,47 Mg:12,75 Ca:109,48 Fe:0,33 Zn:0,5 Col.:10,69
Hsr.:13,46

Quantity of ingredients:
Mozzarella 1 piece / 50g. (yes)
Tomato 2 pieces / 100g. (yes)
Salt 1 pinch / 1g. (little)
Basil (fresh) 5 leaves / 6g. (yes)
Olive oil 2 table spoons / 20g. (yes)
White bread (wheat bread) 2 slices / 40g. (little)

Cooking instructions:
Cut tomatoes and mozzarella into slices. Serve with salt, basil and olive oil. Serve with white bread.

9.81 Turkey breast with vegetables (Asian)

Strengthens blood, strengthens bone marrow, dissolves stagnation, promotes digestion and is goo to fight high blood pressure. Rice to drain the body at overweight and high blood pressure.
Cooking time approx. 45 min
Allergens: AEN
2 portions to 371g. / 535kcal. - (carb:54% / prot:46%)
100g.=144,2kcal. / protein 31,92g. fat:18,02g.
µg. - Ph:27,73 Na:66,82 Ka:46,74 Mg:7,57 Ca:3,14 Fe:0,2 Zn:0,21 Col.:4,05 Hsr.:15,18

Quantity of ingredients:
Rice variety any 1 cup / 120g. (yes)
Water 6 cups / 240g. (yes)
Turkey breast meat 5/8 oz / 200g. (yes)
Ginger fresh 1/3 inch / 3g. (yes)
Garlic 1 piece / 2g. (yes)
Soy sauce 2 table spoons / 20g. (yes)
Wheat flour 2 teaspoons / 15g. (yes)
Onion (spring onion) 2 pieces / 40g. (yes)
Peppers 1/2 piece / 10g. (yes)
Champignon 8 pieces / 30g. (yes)
Sesame oil 2 table spoons / 20g. (yes)
Soy sauce 1 table spoon / 12g. (yes)
Curry 1 pinch / 2g. (yes)
Turmeric (yellow root) 1 pinch / 2g. (rec.)
Chili (pod or ground) 1 pinch / 1g. (yes)
Cashews 2 teaspoons / 25g. (yes)

Cooking instructions:
Cook the rice in salted water.
Cut the turkey meat into thin strips. Peel and dice the ginger and garlic. Put together with the meat strips in a bowl. Mix 1 tbsp of soy sauce with the wheat starch and stir until smooth. Add to the meat and marinate for 30 minutes. Wash spring onions and peppers, clean and cut into small pieces. Clean and quarter the mushrooms. Put one tablespoon of sesame oil in a pan and sauté and warm the marinated turkey. Now add the remaining oil to the pan and fry the other vegetables in it. Now add the meat and season with soy sauce and spices. Serve with the rice. Sprinkle the cashews over the dish before serving.

9.82 Vegetable juice

Promotes digestion, helps to digest fat, supports urination, reduces blood pressure, strengthens immune system, prevents cancer, reduces radiation damage, forcing spleen, is stimulating.
Cooking time approx. 15 min
Allergens: L
1 portion to 225g. / 64kcal. - (carb:82% / prot:18%)
100g.=28,44kcal. / protein 2,46g. fat:0,44g.
µg. - Ph:33,92 Na:30,92 Ka:205,63 Mg:13,57 Ca:34,59 Fe:1,17 Zn:0,33 Col.:0 Hsr.:19,76

Quantity of ingredients:
Celery root 1/2 oz / 20g. (yes)
Carrot 1/4 lbs - 4oz / 100g. (yes)
Tomato 1/4 lbs - 4oz / 100g. (yes)
Garlic 1 piece / 2g. (yes)
Salt 1 teaspoon / 2g. (little)
Acerola fruit nectar or powder 1/2 teaspoon / 1g. (little)

Cooking instructions:
Peel all ingredients and use the juicer to make a drink. Stir in the acerola.

9.83 Vegetable miso soup with tofu

Very powerful, strengthens after febrile illness, reduces blood pressure, strengthens immune system, improves blood circulation, strengthens liver and kidney, detoxifying, strengthens the muscles, reduces flatulence, forcing spleen.
Cooking time approx. 15 min
Allergens: EN
4 portions to 247,75g. / 107kcal. - (carb:22% / prot:78%)
100g.=43,09kcal. / protein 1,85g. fat:9,4g.
µg. - Ph:3,92 Na:13,88 Ka:10,98 Mg:1,98 Ca:4,08 Fe:0,07 Zn:0,01 Col.:0 Hsr.:1,45

Quantity of ingredients:
Sesame oil 2 table spoons / 35g. (yes)
Onion (shallot) 1 piece / 20g. (yes)
Carrot 1 piece / 70g. (yes)
Leek 2 inches / 10g. (yes)
Water 3 cups / 750g. (yes)
Endive salad 2 table spoons / 30g. (yes)
Soy Tofu 2 table spoons / 30g. (yes)
Ginger fresh 1/2 teaspoon / 1g. (yes)
Miso 2 table spoons / 15g. (yes)

Cooking instructions:
In sesame oil first sauté onions, then carrots and a little leek; Pour in water and simmer gently; add the bean sprouts and endive leaves and leave to stand; Tofu cubes, add a little ginger; at the end stir in a little cooled cooking-water the Miso.

9.84 Vegetable rice

Forcing spleen, dissolves stagnation, promotes weight loss. Good to fight immunodeficiency, loss of appetite, flatulence, high blood pressure, strengthens kidney and bladder. Diuretic, warming the body from the inside, regulates internal organs functions.
Cooking time approx. 30 min
Allergens: L
3 portions to 274,67g. / 304kcal. - (carb:88% / prot:12%)
100g.=110,56kcal. / protein 8,1g. fat:3,4g.
µg. - Ph:11,8 Na:1,92 Ka:15,55 Mg:11,36 Ca:27,38 Fe:0,16 Zn:0,07 Col.:0 Hsr.:5,17

Quantity of ingredients:
Broccoli 1/8 lbs - 2oz / 50g. (yes)
Carrot 1/8 lbs - 2oz / 50g. (yes)
Kohlrabi 1/8 lbs - 2oz / 50g. (yes)
Cauliflower 1 oz / 30g. (yes)
Peas 1/2 oz / 20g. (yes)
Margarine 1 teaspoon / 4g. (little)
Rice (whole grain) 5/8 oz / 200g. (yes)
Basic recipe for a vegetable soup (nutritious) 7/8 lbs / 400g. (yes)
Parsley 1/2 oz / 20g. (yes)
Pepper (ground) 1 pinch / 0,2g. ()

Cooking instructions:
Cut the broccoli, carrots and kohlrabi into small cubes, divide the cauliflower into small florets. Heat the margarine in a pan or saucepan, sauté the vegetables. Then add the rice, top up with the vegetable stock and leave to soak for 15-20 minutes.

In the meantime, finely chop the parsley. After cooking, season the rice with freshly ground pepper and parsley.

9.85 Vegetable semolina soup

Diuretic, harmonizes the stomach and intestines, conducts bowel winds, reduces blood pressure, lowers cholesterol, detoxifying, good to fight loss of appetite, flatulence, inflammatory bowel disease, heartburn, twelffinger intestinal ulcers. Stimulates digestion, reduces pain.
Cooking time approx. 20 min
Allergens: AEGL
3 portions to 459,67g. / 199kcal. - (carb:79% / prot:21%)
100g.=43,22kcal. / protein 6,38g. fat:7,02g.
µg. - Ph:4,26 Na:4,63 Ka:23,27 Mg:6,33 Ca:22,08 Fe:0,09 Zn:0,04 Col.:0,39 Hsr.:2,88

Quantity of ingredients:
Basic recipe for a vegetable soup (nutritious) 2 cup / 500g. (yes)
Potato 1 piece / 80g. (yes)
Parsnip 1 piece / 180g. (yes)
Carrot 1 piece / 120g. (yes)
Celery root 3/8 lbs - 6oz / 150g. (yes)
Kohlrabi 1/2 piece / 200g. (yes)
Beans (green, fresh) 1/4 lbs / 100g. (yes)
Wheat semolina 2 table spoons / 24g. (yes)
Lovage 1/2 teaspoon / 2g. (yes)
Butter organic 1 table spoon / 20g. (little)
Soy sauce 1 teaspoon / 3g. (yes)

Cooking instructions:
Worm the prepared vegetable soup; cook the vegetables in the soup softly. Spread some wheatgrass and let it swell. At the end, add lovage-green and a little butter and taste with soy sauce.

9.86 Vitamin drink

Regulates gastrointestinal function, promotes spleen and liver, reduces blood pressure, strengthens immune system, prevents cancer, reduces radiation damage, supports urination, quenches thirst, calms the stomach, prevents cancer.
Cooking time approx. 5 min
3 portions to 273,33g. / 172kcal. - (carb:92% / prot:8%)
100g.=62,93kcal. / protein 2,78g. fat:0,57g.
µg. - Ph:9,44 Na:2,63 Ka:80,69 Mg:7,39 Ca:10,06 Fe:0,28 Zn:0,03 Col.:0 Hsr.:6,17

Quantity of ingredients:
Orange juice 1 cup / 300g. (little)
Carrot 5/8 oz / 200g. (yes)
Banana 2 pieces / 300g. (yes)
Kiwi 1 piece / 20g. (yes)

Cooking instructions:
Chop oranges, carrots, bananas and kiwi and finely puree with the blender.

9.87 Yogurt with honey and nuts

Relieves pain, detoxifying, promotes wound healing. Good to fight acute or chronic constipation of the intestine. Dissolves stones.
Cooking time approx. 5 min
Allergens: GH
1 portion to 167g. / 258kcal. - (carb:61% / prot:39%)
100g.=154,49kcal. / protein 6,79g. fat:12,43g.
µg. - Ph:107,54 Na:38,83 Ka:167,29 Mg:19,4 Ca:104,46 Fe:0,49 Zn:0,54 Col.:10,48
Hsr.:2,16

Quantity of ingredients:
Yogurt (natural, 3.5% fat) 1/4 lbs - 4oz / 125g. (yes)
Honey 2 table spoons / 30g. (little)
Walnuts 1 table spoon / 12g. (yes)

Cooking instructions:
Mix yoghurt with honey and finely chopped nuts.

9.88 Zucchini semolina cream soup

Good to fight loss of appetite, reduces blood pressure, promotes weight loss. Good to fight loss of appetite, flatulence, inflammatory bowel disease, rheumatism, heartburn.
Cooking time approx. 25 min
Allergens: AGL
4 portions to 341,75g. / 146kcal. - (carb:78% / prot:22%)
100g.=42,72kcal. / protein 4,02g. fat:7,8g.
µg. - Ph:1,7 Na:0,83 Ka:9,09 Mg:4,88 Ca:18,35 Fe:0,08 Zn:0,02 Col.:0,22 Hsr.:0,82

Quantity of ingredients:
Butter organic 1/2 oz / 20g. (little)
Wheat semolina 2 table spoons / 20g. (yes)
Parsley 1 Bunch / 100g. (yes)
Basic recipe for a vegetable soup (nutritious) 3 1/2 cups / 800g. (yes)

Lovage 1/2 teaspoon / 2g. (yes)
Nutmeg 1 pinch / 0,5g. (yes)
Anise (Common Fennel) 1 pinch / 0,5g. (yes)
Zucchini 7/8 lbs / 400g. (yes)
Ginger fresh 1/2 teaspoon / 1g. (yes)
Crème fraiche cheese 2 table spoons / 20g. (little)
Lemon peel 1/4 piece / 2g. (yes)
Salt 1 pinch / 1g. (little)
Pepper (ground) 1 pinch / 0,5g. ()

Cooking instructions:
Melt the butter in a saucepan, add the semolina and fry briefly while
stirring. Add half of the chopped parsley, sauté for a short time, pour
vegetable broth according to the basic recipe, season with chopped
lovage, nutmeg and anise. Cook the soup without lid lightly for 10
minutes. Add the finely chopped zucchini and the small piece of lemon
zest, cook gently for 5 minutes until the zucchini are tender. Remove
the lemon peel.
Using the blender, finely puree the soup with the crème fraiche and the
remaining parsley

10 Effects of food

10.1 Use ingredients: recommendable

Leaf salads (bitter)
Lettuce

Turmeric (yellow root)

10.2 Use ingredients: yes

Adzuki beans
Agar agar (kelp)
Agrimony
Almond
Almond milk
Almond puree
Aloe juice
Amaranth
Amaranth Pops
Anchovy / Sardine
Angelica root
Anise (Common Fennel)
Apple (sour)
Apple (sweet)
Apple puree
Apricot
Apricots
Arrowroot
Artichoke
Asparagus (green or white)
Aubergine
Baking powder
Balm
Bamboo shoots
Banana
Banana (cooking banana)
Banchatee (green tea)
barberry
Barley
Barley flour
Barley grass powder
Barley grouts
Barley malt
Barley not peeled
Basic recipe for a beef soup
Basic recipe for a beef soup (warming)
Basic recipe for a chicken soup
(warming)
Basic recipe for a duck soup
Basic recipe for a fish soup
Basic recipe for a rice soup (Congee)
Basic recipe for a vegetable soup
(nutritious)
Basil

Basil (fresh)
Batavia
Bay leaf
Bean oil
Beans (green, fresh)
Bearberry leaf
Beef bone marrow
Beef fillet
Beef heart
Beef heart (calf)
Beef lungs (calf)
Beef meat
Beef meat (calf)
Beef meatbones
Beef Oxtail pieces
Beef soup meat
Beef stomach
Berries of the season
Bitter Herb liqueur
Bitter melon
Bitter orange peel
Black beans
Black caraway
Black fungus mushroom
Black tea
Blackberry dried (unripe fruit)
Blackberry leaves
Blackberry´s
Black-eyed peas
Blackthorn (Sloe)
Blue mallow tee
Blueberry
Blueberry dried
Bocksdorn fruits (Fructus Lycii, goji
berry dried
Boletus mushroom
Borage
Borage oil
Boxhorn clover seeds
Brazil nuts
Bread with carob kernel flour
Breadcrumbs (wheat bread, bread roll)
Brie cheese
Broad beans (thick beans)

Broccoli
Brussels sprouts
Buckbean
Buckwheat
Buckwheat (roasted) Kasha
Buckwheat whole grain
Bulgur (cereals)
Burdock root tea
Bush beans
Butter (half fat)
Butter beans white
Buttermilk
Calamari
Camembert
Cantaloupe
Capers in olive oil
Carambola (Star fruit)
Cardamom
Carob flour, St. john's bread
Carp
Carrot
Carrot (Early Carrot)
Carrot juice without sugar
Cashews
Cauliflower
Caviar
Celery root
Celery sticks
Cereal coffee
Chamomile
Champignon
Channa-Dal
Chanterelle
Chard
Chenpi (chinese tangerine bowl)
Cherry
Cherry (sour)
Cherry compote
Chervil
Chervil dried
Chestnuts
Chicken Blood
Chicken egg
Chicken egg white
Chicken heart
Chicken meat
Chicken stomach
Chicken yolk
Chickpeas
Chickweed
Chicory
Chili (pod or ground)
Chinese cabbage
Chinese pearl barley

Chives
Chlorella (fresh water)
Chrysanthemum blossom tea
Cinnamon ground
Cinnamon sticks
Clementine
Clementines
Clove
Cocoa
Coconut flakes
Coconut grated
Coconut meat
Coconut milk
Cod
Codfish
Coffee
Coix (seeds) YiYi Ren
Cola drink (low calorie)
Compote (fruits of the season)
Cooking oil
Coriander
Coriander (fresh)
Corn
Corn (fast polenta)
Corn (roasted)
Corn flour
Corn germ oil
Corn Grease (Polenta)
Corn silk tea
Corn starch
Cottage cheese
Couscous
Cow's milk (1.5% fat)
Cow's milk (whole milk 3.5% fat)
Crab
Cranberries
Cranberry
Cranberry
Cranberry juice
Cream 10% coffee cream
Cream sour 10%
Creamer
Cress
Crispbread
Crucian
Cucumber
Cucumber (spicy cucumber)
Cumin (Caraway seed)
Curcuma
Curd cheese 20%
Currant (black)
Currant (red)
Currant (white)
Currants (black)

Currants (red)
Curry
Curry paste red
Daisy
Dandelion (young plants)
Dandelion juice
Dandelionroots tea
Dashi
Dates red
Deer meat
Deer meat
Deer's Bones
Deer's kidneys
Dill
Duck (heart)
Duck (slaughtered)
Ducks egg
Dulse (seaweed)
Dyer's broom herb
Edam cheese
Elderberries
Elderberry blossom tee
Emmental cheese
Endive salad
Evening primrose oil
Fennel
Fennel seeds ground
Fennel tea
Fenugreek (Trigonella foenum-graecum)
Feta cheese
Feta cheese
Fig
Fish innards
Fish pieces mixed (fresh water)
Fish remains
Fish sauce
Flounder
Flower pollen
Fox nut, gorgon nut, makhana
French beans
Fresh cheese
Fresh cheese from soya
Fresh cheese with herbs
Freshwater crab
Freshwater fish
Fruit tea
Gail plum
Galangal
Garam Masala powder
Garlic
Gelatin white
Gelee Royal
Gentian root

Ginger fresh
Ginger oil
Ginger powder
Ginkgo fruit
Ginseng root
Goat
Goat and sheep's blood
Goat and sheep's brain
Goat and sheep's milk
Goat and sheep's stomach
Goat cheese
Goose blood
Goose egg
Gooseberry
Gouda cheese
Gourd
Grape juice red
Grape juice white
Grapefruit (Pomelo)
Grapefruit dried peel
Grapefruit juice
Grapeseed oil
Grass carp
Green spelt
Green tea
Greengage
Ground
Ground caraway
Guava
Halibut (Flatfish)
Hawthorn
Hazelnuts
Herbal tea mix
Herbs bitter
Herbs of Provence
Herbs various
Herbs wild
Herring
Hibiscus
Hibiscus tea
Hijiki
Hokkaido pumpkin
Hop
Horehound leaves
Horse meat
Hyssop
Iceberg lettuce
Jasmine blossoms tee
Jellyfish
Juniper berry
Kaki plum
Kalmus
Kefir
Kidney beans (red)

King Solomon's-seal
Kiwi
Kohlrabi
Kombu seaweed (Saccharina japonica)
Kukicha tea
Kumquats
Lamb bones
Lamb meat
Lamb shoulder
Lamb's lettuce
Lamb's lettuce
Lavender blossoms
Leek
Lemon
Lemon Balm (dried)
Lemon Balm (fresh)
Lemon juice
Lemon peel
Lemongrass
Lentils
Lentils black
Lentils red
Lentils yellow
Licorice root tea
Lima beans
Lime
Lime blossom tea
Linseed
Linseed (crushed)
Linseed oil
Liver smoothing tea
Lobster
Longane
Loquate / Japanese medlar
Lotus roots
Lotus seeds
Lovage
Lovage seeds
Luo Han Guo fruit
Lychee
Lychee in Preserved
Lye roll
Mackerel
Mallow (Malva sylvestris) blossom tea
Malt
Mango
Manioc flour
Maple syrup
Mare's milk
Marjoram
Mediterranean fish (cod, plaice,
haddock, sea eel, mackerel)
Medlar
Millet

Millet flakes
Mineral water
Mirabelle plum
Miso
Miso black (fermented)
Miso paste (soy bean paste)
Mixed Pickles
Mold cheese
Morel (black, dried)
Morel, dried
Mozzarella
Mu Erh Mushroom
Muesli
Mulberry fruit
Mulled Wine Spice
Mullet
Multi-grain bread (gray bread)
Mung bean
Mung bean sprouting
Mussels
Mustard
Mustard Dijon
Mustard medium hot
Mustard seeds
Mustard sweet
Mutton
Mutton
Nasturtium (nose-twister or nose-
tweaker)
Nectarine
Nettles
Noodles (wheat) with egg
Noodles (wheat, lasagne) with egg
Noodles (wheat, ribbon noodles) with
egg
Noodles (wheat, spaghetti) with egg
Noodles (whole grain) with egg
Nori, purple seaweed, red algae
Nutmeg
Oat
Oat flakes (whole grain)
Oat flakes roasted
Oat flour
Oat fusion (baby food)
Oat meal
Oat milk
Octopus
Octopus
Okra
Olive oil
Olives
Olives green
Onion (shallot)
Onion (spring onion)

Onion read
Onion white
Orange
Orange blossom
Orange dried peel
Orange grated peel
Orange peel
Oregano dried
Oregano fresh
Oyster mushroom
Oyster shell powder
Oysters
Palm oil
Papaya
Parsley
Parsley root
Parsnip
Passion blossoms tea
Passion fruit
Peaches
Peaches (canned)
Peanut oil
Peanuts
Pear
Pearl barley
Pearl barley
Peas
Peas, green
Pepper Cayenne
Pepper powder (hot)
Pepper white (ground)
Peppercorns
Peppermint
Peppermint tea
Pepperoni
Pepperoni, red, pitted, halved
Pepperoni, yellow, pitted, halved
Peppers
Peppers (rose peppers)
Peppers (sweet)
Peppers powder
Perch
Pheasant
Pickle
Pig blood
Pigeon
Pigeon egg
Pimento
Pine nuts
Pineapple
Pineapple juice without sugar
Pinto beans speckled
Pistachios
Plaice

Plum
Plum dried
Plums
Pomegranate
Poppy
Pork Bacon
Pork brain
Pork ham
Pork ham cooked
Pork ham smoked
Pork heart
Pork knuckle
Pork lung
Pork marrow bones
Pork meat
Pork skin
Pork stomach
Pork/beef sausage (smoked)
Pork's intestine
Potato
Potato (mealy)
Potato flour
Prickly pear
Processed cheese 12%
Psyllium seed
Pudding powder vanilla
Pumpernickel (dark bread)
Pumpkin
Pumpkin seed oil
Pumpkin seeds
Quail
Quail egg
Quince
Quinoa
Rabbit
Rabbit (wild)
Rabbit meat
Radicchio
Radish
Radish (white, green, purple-red)
Radish black
Radish horseradish
Radish leaves
Rapeseed oil
Raspberry
Raspberry dried (immature)
Raspberry leaf tea
Red beet
Red berry (without sugar)
Red cabbage
Reishi mushroom
Rhubarb
Ribworttea
Rice (fragrance)

Rice (Gaoliang / Sorghum)
Rice (whole grain)
Rice Basmati
Rice black
Rice flour
Rice long grain rice
Rice malt
Rice mash
Rice noodles
Rice red
Rice round grain
Rice starch
Rice sticky
Rice sweet
Rice variety any
Rice wild (nature rice)
Romaine lettuce / lettuce salad
Rose blossom tea
Rose hip
Rose hip tea
Rose leaf tea
Rosefish
Rosemary
Rusk
Rye
Rye flour
Rye wholemeal bread
Safflower (Dyer's thistle / Hong Hua)
Saffron
Sage
Sago (cereals)
Sake
Salmon
Salsify
Sauerkraut (cutted cabbage fermented)
Savory
Savoy cabbage / kale
Sea buckthorn
Sea cucumber
Seacrab
Sesame oil
Sesame oil roasted
Sesame paste (Tahini)
Sesame, black
Sesame, white
Shark
Sheep's milk
Sheep's milk yoghurt
Shiitake, dried
Shrimp
Shrimps
Skim milk powder
Slug
Sorrel

Sour cherries
Sour milk
Sour milk cheese 20%
Sourdough
Soy flour
Soy noodles
Soy sauce
Soy Tofu
Soy Tofu smoked
Soya Cuisine (soy cream)
Soybean milk
Soybean oil
Soybeans
Soybeans, black
Soybeans, blacks, fermented
Soybeans, yellow
Spelled (Dark) bread
Spelled flakes
Spelled grain
Spelled semolina
Spelled wholemeal flour
Spinach
Spiny lobsters
Spurdog (spiny dogfish, Schillerlocken)
St. Benedict's thistle, blessed thistle,
holy thistle, spotted thistle
Star anise
Stevia (candyleaf, sweetleaf)
Strawberries
Sugar fructose - fruit sugar
Sugar glucose - grapes sugar
Sugar Milk Sugar
Sugar substitute (sweetener)
Sunflower oil
Sunflower seeds
Sweet potato
Tabasco
Tangerine
Tarragon (Estragon)
Tea mixture uric acid lowering
Thistle oil
Thyme
Thyme dried
Toast bread (whole grain)
Tomato
Tomato dried
Tomato juice
Tomato paste
Tomato puree
Tonic Water
Trout
Trout (smoked)
Truffle
Tsampa (roasted barley flour)

Tuna
Turkey breast meat
Turkey ham
Turnip
Turnips
Umeboshi paste
Umeboshi plums (Japanese apricots)
Valerian
Vanilla pod
Vanilla powder
Vegetable juice
Vinegar (Apple vinegar)
Vinegar (Red wine vinegar)
Vinegar Aceto Balsamico
Vinegar Aceto Balsamico white
Wakame
Walnut oil
Walnuts
Water
Water hot
Watermelon
Wax gourd
Wheat
Wheat bran
Wheat bulgur
Wheat flakes
Wheat flour
Wheat flour whole grain

Wheat germ oil
Wheat semolina
Wheat semolina for children
Wheat/Rye/Gray-black bread with yeast
Wheatgrass juice
Wheatgrass powder
Whey
White beans
White cabbage
Whitefish
Whole grain bread
Wholemeal flour
Wild boar meat
Wild garlic (garlic spinach)
Wild herbs
Wild strawberries
Wormwood herb
Yam root, yam root tuber
Yarrow
Yarrow tea
Yeast
Yew nut
Yoghurt vanilla
Yogi tea
Yogurt (natural, 1.5% fat)
Yogurt (natural, 3.5% fat)
Zucchini

10.3 Use ingredients: little

Acerola fruit nectar or powder
Agave nectar
Almond marzipan
Apple juice (natural cloudy)
Apricot dried
Apricot jam
Apricot nectar
Apricots juice
Avocado
Beef kidney
Beef liver
Beer (alcohol-free)
Beer (alcohol-reduced)
Beer (Pils)
Beer (Top-fermented German dark beer)
Berry juice
Bitter Lemon
Bitter liqueur
Blackberry jam
Blueberry jam
Blueberry juice

Bread roll
Brown ale
Butter organic
Campari
Cherry juice
Chicken liver
Chocolate
Chocolate (Diabetic)
Clarified butter
Coconut fat
Cola drink
Cranberry jam
Cream (30% fat)
Cream sour 20%
Cream sour 30%
Cream, sweet 30%
Créme fraiche cheese
Curd cheese 40%
Currant jam (black)
Currant jam (red)
Currant juice (black)
Dates dried

Eel
Eel smoked
Fernet Branca (herbal bitter liqueur)
Fig dried
Fructose (glucose)
Fruit mix juice
Ginseng liqueur
Goat and sheep's liver
Goose
Goose fat
Goose parts
Gorgonzola
Grapes red
Grapes white
Honey
Honey wine (Met)
Ladyfingers
Lamb kidneys
Lamb liver
Lychee liqueur
Mango juice
Margarine
Margarine (diet)
Martini
Mayonnaise 50%
Mayonnaise 80%
Orange jam
Orange juice
Parmesan
Peanut (roasted)
Peanut butter
Pear juice
Pineapple (from a can)
Pork fat (lard)
Pork kidneys
Pork Lard
Pork liver

Pork sausage (Bratwurst) processed cheese 30%
Prosecco
Puff pastry
Rabbit liver
Raisins
Raspberry jam
Red wine
Rum
Salt
Salt (herbal)
Sherry (whine)
Sour cream 15% fat
Spirit
Strawberry jam
Strawberry Juice
Sugar - icing sugar
Sugar brown
Sugar candy white
Sugar cane sugar
Sugar molasses
Sugar palm sugar
Sugar white
Vanilla
Vanilla sugar natural
Walnuts roasted
Wheat beer
Wheat flatbread/pita bread
White bread (baguette)
White bread (pretzel sticks)
White bread (roll)
White bread (wheat bread)
White breadcrumbs
White dumpling bread (wheat bread cut into chunks)
White wine
Wormwood

10.4 Do not use contra-acting foods

Supplementary nutrition

11 Complementary

11.1 Aniseed

Pimpinelle anisum
preparation: Healing tea (infusion)
Increases bile secretion, positive in hercemias, recommended for bile and liver diet, anti-flatulence, strengthens stomach, good by coughing,

asthma. Promotes milk secretion.

3 teaspoons per cup

Active ingredients: salicylic acid, creosol, alpha-pinene, trans-anethole, fatty oil, sugar, protein.

A hot infusion (infus) is used because of its mucolytic action as a coughing agent due to cramping and bloating action even in gastrointestinal complaints. Anise is therefore often also mixed with fennel and caraway against digestive problems, flatulence, colic and convulsions.

11.2 Artemisia

Artemisiae Argyi, Folium

preparation: Cooking addition

Reduces bleeding, alleviates pain. In the kitchen, mugwort is used as a spice for fat food. Since it contains many bitter substances, it boosts fat burning and promotes digestion.

3-10 g

Do not use in pregnancy.

11.3 Bath for purification

preparation: Healing bath

A bath for purification (base bath), stimulates the natural regeneration of the skin and thus supports the excretion of acids and metabolic waste. The longer you bathe, the more effective the bath is.

Purification bath additive available at the pharmacy or drugstore.

11.4 Cardus marianus, milk thistle

Silybum marianum

preparation: Different effects

Good for colic, cramps, upper abdominal pain, constipation, liver cirrhosis, fatty liver, pancreatic diseases.

An important liver remedy in western naturopathy, especially for detoxification and as an antitoxin. Rarely used as a tea drug, as important (antitoxic) ingredients are poorly soluble in water.

May be slightly laxative.

11.5 Centaurium (centaury)

Centaurium, herb.

preparation: Healing tea (infusion)

Good against loss of appetite, bloating, anemia, fatigue, fever, gallstones,

liver and gallbladder dysfunction, stomach upset, migraine, heartburn, indigestion, wound healing.
Pour 2 teaspoons of the tea into 250 ml of boiling water and leave for 10 minutes. Then sieve.
Drink 2 to 3 cups per day as needed.
Do not use during stomach ulcers.

11.6 Reishi

Ganoderma lucidum
preparation: Different effects
Regenerates the liver, has a detoxifying and anti-inflammatory effect. Good for chronic hepatitis, swelling, redness and itching. Regulates the immune system, awakens and supports the self-healing powers.
Improves the oxygen saturation of the blood.
As an addition to tea, cocoa or coffee. As capsules, extract, powder or whole mushroom.

11.7 Sorrel

Rumex crispus, rad. / Rumex acetosa herb.
preparation: Different effects
Helps against skin diseases (eczema), itching, ulcers, swollen glands, constipation, liver and gland disease, rheumatic diseases, gout, iron deficiency.
Pour fresh or dried leaves with water and leave to soak for at least ten minutes.
Do not use during pregnancy and lactation.

12 Basics of Nutrition

The basic principles of nutrition described herein are general recommendations. They are not aimed at a specific form of therapy. Recommendations concerning a therapy have priority.

12.1 Nutrition

Regular meals in a relaxed atmosphere. A warm breakfast is considered a good start into the day.
The main meals ought to be taken for lunch – supper in the early evening. Pay attention to feeling hungry or sated: don't eat too much nor remain hungry is the rule
Prepare the meals freshly from natural, regional products. Frozen, heat-conserved, industrially prepared or foodstuffs cooked in the microwave oven are rejected.
Choice of foodstuffs according to the season: more cooling food in summer, more warming food in winter.
Eat cooked food at least twice a day. Food and drinks ought to be lukewarm, never ice-cold or hot.
Raw vegetables, briefly cooked vegetables, freshly squeezed juices and mineral water are not recommended. Milk and dairy products are only included in the diet if they don't cause problems.
Don't use therapeutic recipes over a longer period without consulting your doctor or therapist.

Varied food
Enjoy the diversity of foodstuffs. Characteristics of a balanced nutrition are variety, suitable combination and a balanced quantity of rich and low energy foodstuffs (on one hand avoiding undersupply with essential nutrients and on the other hand to take to many undesirable substances).

A lot of Cereal Products - and Potatoes
Bread, pasta, rice, cereal flakes (best wholemeal) as well as potatoes contain almost no fat, but many vitamins, mineral nutrients, trace elements, roughage and secondary plant substances. These foodstuffs ought to be taken with low-fat side dishes.

Vegetables and Fruit – „Take Five" every day …
5 portions of vegetables and fruit a day, as fresh as possible, briefly cooked, or maybe one portion as a juice – ideal as a side dish to every meal as well as snack between meals: Thus a lot of vitamins, mineral nutrients as well as roughage and secondary plant substances

Daily milk and dairy products
Milk and Dairy Products every Day, once or twice per Week Fish; meat, sausages as well as eggs moderately. These foodstuffs contain valuable nutrients like calcium in the milk, iodine selenium and omega-3 fat acids in saltwater fish. Meat is favorable due to its high content of disposable iron and the vitamins B1, B6 and B12. Quantities of 300 – 600 g meat and sausage per week are sufficient. Prefer low-fat products, especially in meat- and dairy products.

Low-fat and fatty Foodstuffs
Fat supplies us with essential fat acids and fatty foodstuffs contain also fat-soluble vitamins. Fat is high in energy; therefore much fat in the food may cause overweight, possibly also cancer. Too many saturated fat acids may further a tendency for cardio-vascular diseases in the long term. Prefer vegetable oils and fats (e.g. rapeseed-, olive-, soya-oils and solid fats produced therefrom). Beware of invisible fat in meat- and dairy products, pastry and sweets as well as in fast-food and convenience foods. 70 – 90 g fat per day is sufficient.

Moderately Sugar and Salt
Take sugar and foods/drinks containing various kinds of sugar (e.g. glucose syrup) only occasionally. Use herbs and spices as well as a little salt creatively. Prefer salt containing iodine.

Plenty of Liquids
Water is absolutely essential. Drink 1-2 l liquids every day. Prefer water (with or without gas) and other low-calorie drinks. Alcoholic drinks should not be taken.

Tasty Dishes, carefully cooked
Cook the meals with as low temperatures and as short as possible, using little water and fat – this preserves the original taste, keeps the nutrients intact and prevents the production of harmful compounds.

Take time and enjoy the food
Take your Time and enjoy your Food
Eating consciously helps to eat right. The eye enjoys food, too. It's fun, invites to enjoy varied dishes and stimulates the feeling of satiety.

Watch your Weight and stay in Motion
A balanced diet and a lot of exercise and sport (30 – 60 min/day) are a healthy combination. The right weight furthers well-being and health. Thermals, directional effectiveness, digestive power

There are various criteria for judging the effectiveness of herbs and foodstuffs.

The use of certain herbs and ingredients is based on observations of the effects on the body which these foodstuffs, herbs and spices show after having eaten them. The medical science has developed following system: Every ingredient or herb has a directional effectiveness. Furthermore, there are herbs which have a special effect on certain organs.

The basic condition for a healthy metabolism is to obtain sufficient energy from food and that the digestive process doesn't use too much energy. An easily digestible meal makes content and sated, doesn't cause flatulence and fatigue after the meal. The perfect spices increase the healthiness of our meals. Very often, just small doses of herbs and spices will suffice. They are not used to make us sated, but to help our digestive organs to digest the food.

12.2 Recipes

The recipes list the ingredients to be used and the cooking instructions show how the dish is prepared. The list of ingredients shows the concerned quantities as well as the relevance for the therapy. If you find „less than mentioned", try to comply or find an alternative from the „list of recommended foodstuffs". Mostly it shall result just in a small change of taste when you simply avoid this ingredient.

Mild cooking methods: boiling, stewing, poaching, steaming
Strong cooking methods: barbecuing, roasting, frying, smoking
Balanced cooking methods: deep-frying, baking brick
Deep-freezing and warming in the microwave oven should be avoided (denaturalization).

12.3 Foodstuffs

Foodstuffs have an effect on body and soul like medicinal herbs, only a very much milder one. Dietary advice is mainly based on regional foodstuffs. The knowledge about the effects of each foodstuff and the knowledge, when which foodstuff shall be used, is based on the orthodox school of medicine. Use ecologic-organic products, if possible. As everything should be cooked for a long time due to a better digestability and very rarely eaten raw, the food agrees with everyone.

The classification of the foodstuffs according to their effect on the body is the basis in order to achieve a harmonious status of health.

Dietary advisors do not recommend certain foodstuffs for everyone. The individual diet is tailor-made for the individual constitution.

Buy only fresh and ripe fruit and vegetables. You ought to leave unripe fruit and vegetables and such with brown spots and wilted leaves behind in the market. In this case take deep-frozen goods (never ready-to-serve dishes!). Fruit and vegetables are deep-frozen immediately after harvesting and often contain more vitamins and minerals than the goods from the vegetable shelf. Whereas conserved or tinned goods contain very much less biological substances. Also, salt, sugar and others are mostly added to the latter. Never leave the foodstuffs in the water after washing them to avoid that many vital substances get drowned. Clean salads, fruit and vegetables immediately before serving.

Please make sure of the hygienic processing of foodstuffs. Clean your salads, fruit and vegetables carefully. When cooking with meat, prepare all ingredients first and then process the meat products. Clean the worktop and tools very carefully. Wooden surfaces ought to be treated with a mild disinfectant regularly in order to reduce germination.

Store fruit and vegetables separately, if possible. Harvested fruit and vegetables are still alive and emit e.g. ethylene gas, which makes other products ripen and age faster. Keep meat and fish in the closed packaging or store them in the fridge in closed containers.

12.4 Herbs

There are some basic rules for storing medicinal herbs. On principle, herbs must be protected from direct sunlight, humidity and heat.

Containers for the storage of herbs may be glasses, ceramic jars and even plastic containers. However, plastic is a rather unsuitable material and should only be a short-term solution. In case of glass containers, use a dark material.

Medicinal herbs cannot be kept for any long period. The shelf life of herbs is limited. However, it can be prolonged with suitable storage. The place should be dark, rather cool and absolutely dry. A wooden medicine cabinet, placed not directly next to a source of heat, would be ideal. Never buy large quantities of herbs so as not to have to throw them away. Label the container with the name of the herb and the date of harvesting or processing.

13 Other dietic-books

The following syndromes of dietetics, TCM or for a therapy supplement for cancer are available.

Dietetics

E001. Nutrition of the infant - baby food
E002. Nutrition during lactation
E003. Nutrition in old age
E004. Nutrition of children and adolescents
E005. Nutrition of athletes
E006. Light weight
E007. Pregnancy
E008. Full food

Protein and electrolyte - kidneys
E009. (hemodialysis) dialysis treatment
E010. Acute renal failure
E011. Chronic renal insufficiency
E012. Nephrotic syndrome
E013. Kidney stones (nephrolithiasis)

Gastrointestinal tract - pancreas
E014. Acute pancreatitis (inflammation of the pancreas)
E015. Chronic pancreatitis (inflammation of the pancreas)

Gastrointestinal tract - small intestine and large intestine
E016. Acute obstipation (constipation)
E017. Chronic obstipation (constipation)
E018. Colon irritabile
E019. Diverticulitis
E020. Acquired lactose intolerance (lactose malabsorption)
E021. Fructose malabsorption
E022. Glutensensitive enteropathy (celiac disease)
E023. Colectomy
E024. Short Bowel Syndrome

Gastrointestinal tract - liver, gallbladder, bile ducts
E025. Acute and chronic hepatitis (inflammation of the liver)
E026. Cholelithiasis (bile stones)
E027. fatty liver
E028. cirrhosis

Gastrointestinal tract - Stomach and duodenal intestine
E029. Acute gastritis
E030. Chronic gastritis
E031. Stomach bleeding
E032. Ulcus ventriculi and duodenal ulcer
E033. Condition after gastric surgery

Gastrointestinal tract - oral cavity and esophagus
E034. Stomatitis
E035. Esophageal carcinoma (esophageal cancer)
E036. Refluosophagitis (heartburn)

Special diseases
E037. Phenylketonuria (PKU)
E038. Rheumatic joint diseases

Metabolism
E039. Obesity (overweight)
E040. Diabetes mellitus
E041. Eating disorders (underweight)

Fat metabolism
E042. Hypercholesterolaemia (increased cholesterol level)
E043. Hepatic Encephalopathy

Heart and circulation
E044. Arteriosclerosis (arterial calcification)
E045. Heart insufficiency
E046. Hypertension
E047. Hyperuricaemia and gout

Changed nutrient requirements
E048. In case of fever
E049. For malignant diseases
E050. After burns
E051. Radiation and chemotherapy

CANCER
E100. Pancreatic cancer
E101. Bladder cancer
E102. Blood cancer (leukemia)
E103. Breast cancer
E104. Colorectal cancer
E105. Gastric cancer
E106. Kidney cancer
E107. Esophageal cancer

TCM
E200. Bladder - moisture heat in the bladder
E201. Bladder - moisture and cold in the bladder
E202. Bladder - emptiness and cold in the bladder
E203. Large intestine - external cold affects the large intestine
E204. Large intestine - moisture heat in the large intestine
E205. Large Intestine - heat blocks the intestine II acute
E206. Large intestine - dryness of the colon
E207. Large intestine - Yang deficiency (cold)
E208. Heart - Blood insufficiency
E209. Heart - Blood stagnation
E210. Heart - Fire
E211. Heart - Hot mucus clogs the heart pores

E212. Heart - Cold mucus clogs the heart pores
E213. Heart - Qi deficiency
E214. Heart - Yang deficiency
E215. Heart - Yin deficiency
E216. Liver - Ascending Liver Yang
E217. Liver - Blood deficiency
E218. Liver - Blood stagnation
E219. Liver - Moisture heat in liver and gall bladder
E220. Liver - Fire
E221. Liver - Gall bladder Qi-Empty
E222. Liver - Cold in the liver meridian
E223. Liver - Qi stagnation
E224. Liver - Wind
E225. Liver - Wind with ascending liver Yang
E226. Liver - Wind with blood anemic
E227. Liver - Wind with extreme heat
E228. Lung - Qi deficiency
E229. Lung - Mucus-moisture in the lungs
E230. Lung - Mucus-heat in the lungs
E231. Lung - Mucus-cold in the lungs
E232. Lung - Dryness of the lungs
E233. Lung - Wind-heat attacks the lungs
E234. Lung - Wind-cold affects the lungs
E235. Lung - Yin deficiency
E236. Stomach - Bloodstagnation
E237. Stomach - Fire
E238. Stomach - Cold with liquid
E239. Stomach - Nutrition stagnation
E240. Stomach - Qi deficiency
E241. Stomach - Rebellious Qi
E242. Stomach - Yin Emptiness
E243. Spleen - Heat and moisture attack the spleen
E244. Spleen - Coldness and moisture affects the spleen
E245. Spleen - Qi deficiency
E246. Spleen - Qi deficiency + Declining spleen Qi
E247. Spleen - Qi deficiency + spleen does not control the blood
E248. Spleen - Yang deficiency
E249. Kidney - Heart and kidney no longer communicate
E250. Kidney - Jing deficiency
E251. Kidney - Kidneys cannot receive the Qi
E252. Kidney - Qi is not stable
E253. Kidney - Yang deficiency
E254. Kidney - Yin deficiency

For further information visit di-book.com.

14 EBNS - Software for nutritional counseling

The main task of the database is to create personalized nutritional advice for each patient individually. The database was developed for Dietetics and Traditional Chinese Medicine.

The Database supports training and advices in the daily work routine.

The computer program provides lists of recipes, ingredients and herbs, which are given to the client. individually adjustable according to patient's request from whole food to vegetarians (lacto, ovo, ...). For every register there is an information sheet which can be given to the client. All texts can be individually designed.

The syndromes can be combined and result in an intersection of the recommended recipes and ingredients. The automated diagnosis for the TCM enables you to check your experience during the training as well as to confirm your diagnosis in the working day. You select several predefined symptoms and have the program automatically display the relevant syndromes.

How to work with the database:
Select the patient / client, select one or more of the syndromes you diagnosed and print the folder.

You can change all values, create new symptoms or syndromes, develop recipes, change or adapt ingredients and herbs to your findings. In simple client management, all relevant data about the person is stored. You get an overview of the past diagnoses and the development of the course of the disease.

As a consultant you save a lot of time when you print out the recipe, food and herbal lists for the recognized syndromes and give them to the clients. You can use this time for a personal conversation. With the database, dieticians and nutritionists can view the nutrients and trace elements for each recipe and develop recipes for syndromes even with suggested ingredients.

All recipe and grocery lists can also be ordered from me as a combination of several diseases. I wish all readers good luck, health and happiness in life.
More information can be found at www.ebns.at.
Volunteer: www.krebsinfo.at
Josef Miligui